The Cult
of
the Leader

The Cult
of
the Leader

A Manifesto for More
Authentic Business

Christopher Bones

A John Wiley & Sons, Ltd., Publication

This edition first published 2011
© 2011 Christopher Bones

Registered office
John Wiley & Sons Ltd, The Atrium, Southern Gate, Chichester, West Sussex,
PO19 8SQ, United Kingdom

Under the Jossey-Bass imprint, Jossey-Bass, 989 Market Street, San Francisco CA
94103-1741, USA
www.jossey-bass.com

For details of our global editorial offices, for customer services and for information
about how to apply for permission to reuse the copyright material in this book
please see our website at www.wiley.com.

ISBN 978-0-470-66604-3
A catalogue record for this book is available from the British Library.

Set in 11.5 on 17 pt Jenson Pro by Toppan Best-set Premedia Limited
Printed in Great Britain by TJ International, Padstow, Cornwall

For Hamish and Sophie

Contents

Acknowledgements   ix

Introduction: The Gods that Failed   1

Part One: The Diagnosis   13

1. Practically perfect in every way: The making of the modern leader   15

2. Because we're worth it: The rise of the L'Oreal generation   44

3. Why didn't we see it coming? The loss of liability, stewardship and owner control   67

4. The public gets what the public wants: Values, confidence, trust and reputation in leadership   98

Part Two: The Solutions   125

5. The manifesto for a more authentic business   127

6. Diamonds on the soles of your shoes: The real war for talent   136

7. Moving from warm gestures to cold showers: A
    reframing of executive reward   166

8. Less is more: The future of leadership and its
    development in organizations   202

Conclusion: The importance of being earnest. The price
    of the cult and the value of leadership   229

Index   256

Acknowledgements

There are many people who have contributed to the development of the ideas in this book and whose thinking has shaped and directed my own when I began to reflect on the state of leadership in modern organizations. In particular I would like to thank my colleagues at Henley Business School, and especially Professor Malcolm Higgs, Professor Stephen Lee, Dr Kevin Money, the Director of the John Madejski Centre for Reputation and Phil Radcliff who so successfully leads the Henley Leadership Programme. This book sprang from an original article for 'The Economist.com' which created a worldwide debate about modern leaders and I would like to thank Conrad Heine, the Management Editor of *The Economist* for giving me that opportunity to share my views. Considerable credit for the finished product goes to Ellen Hallsworth at John Wiley & Sons who has been a diligent, thoughtful and supportive editor, always ready to give feedback and advice, understanding of all the aspects of being a business school Dean that got in the way of completion, but never letting up on her determination to ensure the book appeared. Finally I have to thank my wife, Gail, who endured the travails of writing, editing and all the associated frustrations by being an editor, proof reader and as always a great support.

Chris Bones
January 2011

Introduction:
The Gods that Failed

If ever we needed great leadership in the world, then this must be the time that it should come forward and so far the 21st century hasn't really delivered. The global financial crisis, the failure of the world's governments to agree a plan to mitigate our changing climate, the stalemate in the Middle East peace process, the stalling of the 'Darfur' round and the continuing failure to reverse the rise of religious and political fundamentalism have all been ascribed in the media, in books and by polemicists of all persuasions to a common factor: a failure of leadership.

Good leaders would not let these things happen. The weak ones in key positions have, by their actions or inactivity (take your pick), been the authors not just of their own misery but, more importantly, of the conglomeration of crises that we now face. This is to be expected: in adversity we all look for someone to blame and rarely do we look to ourselves. We look to those who we believe have led us into the problem we now face.

The failure of leadership, and the doling out of blame in the aftermath, has had far-reaching consequences. Trust and confidence has bottomed out, not only in the current leaders of business, government, public services, but also in these systems and structures themselves; the systems and structures which have underpinned the way we live for the past fifty or sixty years. In the West, these systems and structures were based on three tenets. The first was that economic growth, measured through increases in gross domestic product was a good thing per se. The second, that consumption of scarce resources to satisfy the end consumer was the single most important outcome for all producers of economic activity be they firms or governments. Thirdly and more recently, that wealth could be better created through short-term changes in asset values rather than through the creation of goods and services that could be sold for a value greater than the cost of their delivery.

The result has been that, in the 21st century the wealthy have so much disposable income that they are able to consume to no real purpose apart from the purpose of consumption itself. The following diagrams (Figure I.1 and Figure I.2) demonstrate the extent to which the wealthiest have benefited in Great Britain[1] over the ten years 1998–2008:[2]

The behaviour and spending patterns of the wealthiest have in themselves become an aspiration for those far less wealthy. Such aspiration was spurred on by political leaders from Reagan and Thatcher to Bush and Blair, who created visions of a property-owning democracy where everyone could own their own home. In this brave new world, the fact of such ownership could make money in itself that could then be spent on furthering their ambitions to ape the lives of celebrities through even more consumption. To fuel these aspirations, business teamed up with the banks to exploit the deregulation of financial services in much of Europe and North America. Easy credit fuelled the emergence of something called 'a lifestyle'.

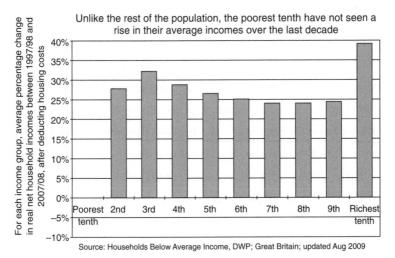

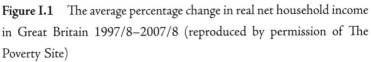

Figure I.1 The average percentage change in real net household income in Great Britain 1997/8–2007/8 (reproduced by permission of The Poverty Site)

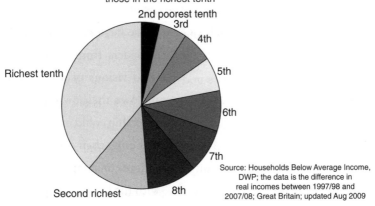

Figure I.2 The difference in income growth between households in Great Britain 1997/8–2007/8 (reproduced by permission of The Poverty Site)

Originally said to be a sociological term coined by Alfred Adler in the 1920s,[3] it is now in common parlance and will in my view become the term that defines the generation for whom consumption became a way of life. Where shopping became a pastime rather than a chore and where those with more money than sense were able to spend on themselves just because they were worth it. This is the L'Oreal generation.

Their leaders were the epitomes of 'lifestyle'. They looked the part, wore the clothes, lived in the houses, drove the cars, invested in the second homes, flashed the credit cards – and plenty of them. They ate in the restaurants, espoused the politics of change, had the cosmetic enhancements and lived their lives of instant gratification. These were the modern pantheon of gods. The gods of capital (exemplified by Sir Fred Goodwin, Kenneth D. Lewis, Lloyd Blankfien amongst others) and the gods of economics (just think of Alan Greenspan, Ayn Rand and Milton Friedman as representing those who drove the pre 2008 orthodoxy). The gods of business (three who spring to mind are Kenneth Lay, WorldCom CEO, Stan O'Neil of Merrill Lynch and Carly Fiorina of HP); the gods of style (we shouldn't forget Martha Stewart or Carole Caplin, or perhaps we should); and the gods of sport (what now for Tiger Woods, Joey Barton and Ben Johnson?). The gods of communication (the rivalries and global ambitions of Rupert Murdoch, Ted Turner and Conrad Black dominated for a decade) and the gods of the politics (Tony Blair, Bill Clinton and Silvio Berlusconi all brought celebrity to politics and took politics to new levels of public contempt) . This generation's fascination with celebrity, and their wish to emulate the latest trend in every aspect of life, made these people international household names, whose every move was watched, reported on and copied. They intermingled (the reports on Tony Blair's and Gordon Brown's guest lists for Chequers,[4] the UK Prime Minister's country retreat, and the reporting on Tony Blair's annual vacations[5] show the intermingling of the political class with film stars, rock icons, billionaires, sports stars and the like) and created a coterie of self-reinforcing role models who met and glittered on a carousel of country houses, yachts, palaces, palazzos, ranches and the occasional dacha.

In one way or another, these are the gods who have failed. The revenge of the L'Oreal generation has already seen some of them into retirement, into obscurity and in a few cases into jail. Most of those who remain will eventually suffer as all false gods do. For the paradise hasn't just been postponed, it will never materialize. The L'Oreal generation has just found out that it will have to work longer, save harder, pay more to the state in taxation and suffer more natural disasters than any generation in living memory. They're going to blame someone.

Some will argue that out of such a melting pot of disaster and change will come forward a new type of leader, someone capable of being different and doing different things. This was the basis of the Obama campaign in 2009 and it is already possible to see opposition leaders in other countries adopting this proposition as a potential vote-winning strategy. At the same time the old way of doing things is already rearing its head again, in banking, in politics, in business and in public services. It doesn't seem like leaders have learned very much from what has happened.

Perhaps all they need to do is to read the books and find the answer: there are more than enough of them. More than 1.9 million business books are now offered by Amazon, including more than

267,000 in the 'business management' category. In 2009 11,000 business books were published in the United States alone. To give you some sense of scale apparently if they were placed one on top of another, the stack would stand as tall as a nine-story building.[6] One way or another, a significant part of the canon deals with one topic: how we can become great leaders. Solutions are proffered from every angle. Academic research looks to correlate success against identified and defined behavioural characteristics. Consultants exhort us to adopt practices based on the experiences of successful leaders; and there are the lessons we can extract from fiction written up by self-styled leadership gurus.

Regardless of the credibility or otherwise of the source for such recipes for success, these books all claim to provide an answer to leadership perfection. They stem from a tradition which believes that empirical study can demonstrate what it takes to succeed. All that is required is for individuals to adopt new ways of being and doing for us to change.

This book is written from a different perspective: it argues that no-one can become the perfect leader because no such thing exists. Indeed, I go further, to say that the cult that now surrounds leadership and leader development is positively dangerous, not just for business but for society as a whole.

All leaders are flawed because all human beings are flawed. Saints are rare (and equally capable of human failure[7]). Indeed, in the Christian tradition, we are all born with sin and are capable of it. Regardless of how good we strive to be, we will commit sufficient sin to warrant confession and to plead for forgiveness at least once a week. In the more contemplative traditions human flaws are accepted as given and whilst the most religious are those who have striven hardest to eradicate their human failings, the vast majority recognize and accept that they are imperfect. The shared ambition, however, in these philosophies is the search for well-being in a spiritual as well as material sense.[8]

The lessening of the importance of the thinking behind religious traditions in education in the West has removed this reinforcement of imperfection from many lives. Leaders are subject to breathless adoration from 'puff pieces' in the mass media. They are surrounded by armies of image consultants and spin doctors. Cultures of compliance at the top of organizations are driven by the access to untold wealth that can be endowed upon people from very ordinary backgrounds if they stay 'in' with the boss for long enough. All this has created conditions in many modern organizations more akin to a feudal court than a collective of equals within which freely held views and opinions can be shared without fear.

This modern leader is egoistic, blind to their own faults, surrounded by people created in their own image and committed to actions driven more by the need to enhance their self-image than by anything else. We moved from ranking *companies* and their performance to personalizing such comparative exercises by focusing on their CEOs, as though the CEO was the defining differentiator without which the organization would not have achieved their success. The UK's 'Most Admired Companies' awards describe themselves as 'The UK's Business Oscars'[9] and lionize the CEOs whose organizations are placed in the top spots. The gods of business: Jack Welch, Lee Iacocca, Bernard Arnault, Niall FitzGerald, Donald Trump, Lord Sugar of Clapton, Jack Ma, Sir John Harvey-Jones, Sir Gerry Robinson, Sir Richard Branson, Lord Browne and more are lionized, attended to with reverence, and placed on pedestals from which they pronounce on the issues of the day. Many have become best-selling authors, chat show guests, and even hosts of their own prime-time television shows. Some even made it, albeit briefly, into government. With all this adoration can you blame them for believing in their own immortality? Can you blame others for working hard to join them in the ranks of the deified?

Once at this level these people (and despite what is said there are women in this group as well as men) see themselves as Titans. Just as with the ancients, heaven help anyone who inadvertently gets in the way when Titans clash: just ask the shareholders of the Royal Bank of Scotland about the acquisition of ABN-AMRO. This takeover battle swiftly became a test of strength. For RBS when faced with Barclays' alternative (and most would argue strategically more sensible) bid. The company's determination to be the winner did possibly even more than their poor banking practice (which would seem no worse in the face of it than that of Barclays), to ensure the eventual nationalization of nearly 85% of the bank.[10]

Some of our greatest moral philosophers have explored leadership and their words resonate powerfully in the detritus of the near-collapse of the financial system. The focus on the role of the leader in society has been at the heart of the development of much of modern political and social thought. It was Aristotle in his *Treatise on Government* who captured the essence of the proposition of the 'altruistic' or 'virtuous' leader:

But since we say that the virtue of the citizen and ruler is the same as that of the good man and that the same person must first be a subject and then a ruler, the legislator has to see that they become good men and by what means this may be accomplished …[11]

For the want of good men (and women) at the top of the world's financial services industry, its regulators and its political leadership the world nearly destroyed the very system that had until recently delivered the progress, social and economic, that has supported over sixty years of comparative peace and prosperity for mankind.

Yet despite this, the globalization of the world's economic systems will continue. In the bigger sweep of history, connecting across boundaries will continue to drive forward a development that, whilst held back or reversed from time to time, seems to be as instinctive to mankind as market-oriented behaviour. As we connect more, as we face the challenges of a more global economic system and of the global challenges presented by a changing climate and an increasingly populous planet, so the problems that need resolution will become increasingly complex and even more global. The need for leaders who can build support to act for the greater good therefore increases rather than diminishes.

In business, just as much as in any other part of society, good men and women are needed to lead their organizations through the challenges they face. Yet today business leaders are as ill-regarded as politicians. At the heart of this ill-regard is a belief that they are overrated, over-powerful and over-paid.

In 2008 Gallup published their annual 'Voice of the People' survey for the World Economic Forum.[12] Carried out during the early stages of the global credit crunch its findings showed a world increasingly worried about the future. The survey, covering sixty countries in the developed and developing world, revealed an increasing level of concern. These concerns covered predictions of a less safe and less prosperous planet alongside rising concern over increasing wars and conflicts, doubts about the global 'war' on terrorism and about the need to protect the environment. It also reflected a continuing trend of mounting distrust in leaders in all walks of life.

Globally, 43% of citizens said that political leaders are dishonest; 37% said they have too much power; 33% said they are unethical; 27% said they are not competent. Whilst Africans 'were the most critical of their politicians' with 81% calling political leaders dishonest, in countries perceived as more stable and openly democratic politicians still fared very badly. More than half of Americans and over two thirds of Austrians and Germans and even 50% of the Swiss felt their leaders were dishonest.

Business leaders, however, fared only marginally better: 34% believed business leaders are dishonest (vs. 43% for politicians); 34% said business leaders have too much power and 30% said they are unethical. 2009 will not have made a positive impact on these perceptions and the continuing refusal of those in senior roles, especially in the financial services sector, to accept these perceptions as valid and requiring action will ensure that business continues to be the focus of public disquiet and mistrust.

These results reflect a crisis of confidence in leaders that is global, worsening and without deliberate action from the top of organizations in all sections of civil society, potentially destabilizing. The crash and the role played by business leaders particularly in creating the climate where the international financial system was taken to the very edge of collapse will accelerate and exacerbate this trend. However, the trend has been there for some time and the potential for nemesis had been flagged, not just by those like me who were uncomfortable with the shift in the values set but also by those with serious platforms to whom serious people listened. Yet if they listened, they cannot have understood the potential for disaster as they did nothing.

In the 2010 World Economic Forum the measure used was the Edelman Trust Barometer and despite the crisis, it would seem that the response so far by business and its leaders has done little or nothing to address this dire state of affairs. Over 60% of the global population said they trusted business less in 2009 than they did in the previous year, with only one major country, India, showing fewer than 50% felt this way. In the UK, France and Germany only 36% of those questioned trusted business. In the US trust in business was not much higher and there were significant falls in trust in two industries: banking and automotive where levels of trust in both roughly halved in a year. This trend was not reflected in emerging economies such as China, Brazil and Indonesia, perhaps reflecting the difference in perceived role and responsibilities.

These overall trends were reinforced when asked if business should face stronger and tougher regulation, with over 60% globally saying that governments should intervene and even nationalize companies to restore trust. Even in the US not even half of those questioned thought the free market should be able to operate independently.[13]

So how on earth did we find ourselves here, and even more importantly what on earth can we do about it? This book explores these issues. In Part One it offers an explanation of why leadership in the latter part of the 20th century became so self-centred and narcissistic. It analyses the impact on public trust in leaders in all sectors and the lack of confidence we have in today's leaders to act in the best interests of the whole as opposed to themselves. In Part Two it turns to thinking about what can be done to change where we are and lays out a radical programme that could transform public perceptions of leaders in today's organizations. For in the end only really radical change can re-set public perceptions. Without it, we lay the seeds for upheaval that could see much of what we have worked hard to achieve swept away. Regardless of country, the current state of public opinion in much of the developed and developing world is driving a resurgence of political movements that want to impose controls on the natural human behaviours that underpin the market as the mechanism through which we create wealth. This desire to restrain or even remove the market mechanism will be accelerated by any continuation of the failure of those responsible for regulation and proper management of the market to address the iniquities of today's leadership class. The cost of a government committed to shackle the market, rather than to regulate it, is far too big a price to pay for a failure to reform. This book offers leaders of business and society a manifesto for change: without these changes it won't just be business that suffers, but society as a whole.

Part One

The Diagnosis

Chapter One
Practically Perfect in Every Way
The Making of the Modern Leader

THE DEVELOPMENT OF THE LEADER

The Modern Leader is, like all of us, a result of inheritance. Our genetic forefathers shaped our physical strengths and weaknesses and our intellectual potential. Much of who we are in these dimensions is as a result of history (and pre-history). What we do with this inheritance, however, is not pre-determined. Today's leaders are the product therefore of two specific things: the historical development of leadership and the environment in which they operate. This chapter deals with the historical development of the cult of the leader, the two that follow will deal with the current environment: combined they present a proposition as to why the modern leader has failed.

In the cult of the leader, history matters. We have an inherited way of living in tribes which is at the heart of the way that we, as a species, have evolved. As with other primates, pecking orders and leadership roles have always been with us. What differentiates us from other primates is our ability for rational thought and as this has developed so we have applied it to leadership as we have to so many other aspects of our lives. From the earliest beginnings of recorded thought man has reflected on the nature of success in leadership. The earliest civilizations recorded and celebrated the achievements of their leaders and in those civilizations where deities took human forms, they too were given attributes associated with the human experience of leaders in real life. Not just in the writings of historians, writers and poets but also in the pictures and sculptures of each tradition we have built through time an image of leaders and their characteristics: whether these were good, bad or indifferent.

Clearly whilst alive, powerful leaders went out of their way to ensure that stories about them and the images that were employed to portray them reinforced their right to lead and the basis of their power. In a world where the majority did not read or write and where brute force, superstition and religion played as much as role in the acceptance of a leader as any sophisticated justification of hereditary, judicial or democratic right, portraiture developed a very significant role in communicating and reinforcing the role of the leader.

Since the early renaissance, art developed a very sophisticated ability to reflect upon the nature of leadership. Arguably this came about initially as a result of patronage in that those with the wealth from positions of economic, social or religious power retained and sponsored artists and in return were portrayed by them in return. Over centuries, as artists continued to be sponsored by the powerful they developed an iconography and a presentation of power that has shaped a significant part of the inheritance of leaders in modern organizations. The history of the representation of the leader in art shows us the degree of conditioning within which leaders have grown up and how the continuing sense of their own position and perspective of many of those in leadership roles has been shaped. Leadership became embodied in a single leader and as the leader became the embodiment of the state so this set the scene for the leader in other contexts to become the embodiment of their own organization.

European art was transformed with the development of new understandings of perspective that transformed the flat, Byzantine-style two dimensional representations of the dark ages into the figurative, three dimensional realism that appeared in the 13th century. Art historians have identified the pioneering techniques of Giotto Di Bondone and his followers as a significant transformation which enabled a shift in subject matter for the visual arts from the predominantly religious to embrace far more realistic representations of the secular. As art techniques progressed and as artists became more sophisticated in their representation of the human condition so they were able to tell much more sophisticated and complex stories in their pictures. Leaders become flattered by those artists whom they patronized and were placed at the heart of society and at its highest point. What finally developed was the presentation of the leader as next only to God, the leader as God's representative on earth, the leader as the embodiment of us all and as above all others bar God. In the 14th and 15th centuries even renaissance leaders in supposedly democratic Florence and other city-states found way of reinforcing themselves as 'primus inter pares' (first amongst equals) whilst later, more autocratic leaders firmly dispensed with this humility and had themselves presented as the apotheosis of human achievement.

Renaissance painters used heavy symbolism to underline the importance of the secular power at a time when the power of the church was significantly greater than that of any secular leader. One of the leading practitioners of this approach was Sandro Botticelli

(c. 1446–1510) and the most famous representation of his approach hangs in the Uffizi gallery in Florence: 'The Adoration of the Kings'. This shows the story of the Christian Holy Family receiving the adoration of the magi. Here, however, is not only an image of a story known by everyone who would have seen the picture when it was first displayed, but also a stark representation of the power and importance of the Medici family, the first and foremost of the merchant princes of Florence. For the magi kneeling at the feet of Christ is the most powerful man in Florence, Cosimo Medici. By placing him next to the Son of God himself Botticelli is telling everyone in Florence to whom they have to pay homage as leader. The representation does not stop here, but goes on to reinforce the power of the dynasty by including in the painting two further generations of Medici: Cosimo's son Piero and grandson Giovanni.[1]

As the renaissance developed its fascination with things classical, the pre-industrial age in Europe often used Greco-Roman or local mythology to portray its kings, generals and grand citizenry in the guise of the Caesars, or with allusions to local and well understood legends such as those from Arthurian, Germanic or Norse tales. As the 18th century progressed so the leader moved from a paragon of virtues associated with Aristotle's leader (learned, artistic, a sportsman as well as a general) to being portrayed as the source of power. The symbols and trappings of the state (crowns, sceptres, orbs, ermine and the like) as representations of the power of armed force came to the fore. So much so that revolutionaries once in possession of power employ exactly the same allusions as those whom they have deposed.

The renaissance leader, informed by the counsel of Machiavelli, developed into a leader who presented himself as the source of all:

'L'Etat c'est moi' said Louis XIV to the Parlement de Paris in 1655.[2] This reflected the philosophical proposition that directly connected kings to God and made them the dispenser of justice, of position in society and ultimately of wealth. He is portrayed in a series of paintings by all of the great artists of the day. The most famous is probably by Henri Testelin (1616–1695) and is an example of how the artist was able to tell this story through a single image. Louis commands his throne with a firm grip on the symbols of power. At his feet is the world, represented by the globe, showing his dominance even over other kings and images of learning, of wisdom (the Greek head) and of scientific understanding (the trigonometry instruments). His hand rests on a child, representing him as the father of the nation as well as the father in the family.

Whilst in England this belief in the inherited right from God of kings to rule without let or hindrance cost Charles I his head and the monarchy its primacy over parliament, in much of Europe this leadership model was reinforced during the latter part of the 18th century by the Hapsburgs, the Hohenzollerns, the Bourbons (in Spain and in France) and the Romanovs. This era of the enlightened autocrat developed the theme of 'father or mother of the nation' acting on behalf of their children as all parents do because they knew best. This leader was benign, a leader who was committed to the well-being of the nation, who was forward-looking and interested in the life of every subject. They were wise and all powerful. For those who accepted this settlement of power within the state the enlightened autocrat protected them from injustice within and from enemies without. They were reformers, yet in no sense were they democrats nor were they interested in sharing power. They controlled the reins of central power and were ruthless in removing privileges from provinces, representative assemblies and religious organizations, especially those associated with taxation or with exercising any degree of control or restraint over the monarch's ability to enact legislation and dispense justice.[3] For those who attacked the state, and the status quo within in it, there was to be neither tolerance nor mercy. They ran highly disciplined police forces and secret services, they employed informers and used their power to imprison without trial, to exile (internally and externally) and to murder. They often ascended their thrones as a result of violence and many died violently. As well as brute force, these leaders employed extravagant display, wealth and external show to demonstrate their power and their permanence. Their courtiers, cardinals and catamites did likewise.

Joseph II of Austria (1741–1790) was arguably the greatest exponent of Enlightened Autocracy. His portrait by Joseph Hickel (1736–1807) is a wonderful example of the development of the cult of the leader in the 18th century. It shows Joseph in his finery, wearing his honours next to a sculpture of Minerva the goddess of wisdom and between them an owl representing knowledge. Here is the leader as all wise, all knowing and all powerful, utilizing these super-human attributes for the good of those he rules over. Despite the shifts in the balance of power between the rulers and the ruled in the intervening two hundred and fifty years and the introduction of the concept of a universal franchise for the appointment of people to executive office the presentation of many modern leaders in all walks of life is not much different.

In some ways this shouldn't surprise us. If one looks at the development of the business leader in generation after generation we can see a progression from the economic radicalism of the entrepreneur to the social conservatism of the respected elder. As societies developed and the ownership of land became the defining attribute of power so those in 'trade' and later in 'production' looked to acquire social standing with the wealth they created. In so doing they aped the pretensions and the practices of those with political and social power in society. The industrial revolution may well have brought a radical shift in power and influence in favour of those who owned capital rather than land, but it didn't change the leadership paradigm. To confirm their status in 18th and 19th century society these newly rich[4] bought estates, acquired aristocratic titles, sat in parliaments and presented themselves as leaders in the same way as those who were born into leadership roles. The acceptability of business came much later to society's leaders than that of the church or parliament or the professions. Whilst no-one could doubt the economic muscle, it was conforming to social norms of leadership status that eventually secured these new men their acceptance. Business leaders shaped themselves in the mould of the formerly omnipotent.

The modern inheritors of this tradition of faithful representation of the person, both in painting and in photography, show the leaders of today as thoughtful, considered and as socially conservative as their predecessors. They sit in solid chairs reminiscent of the thrones of the kings of old. They often hold representations of their power or achievements or appear against backgrounds that tell their story. These representations are used to communicate leadership traits that people want to see: reliability, prudence and trustworthiness. Even with the advent of television and radio these images continue to play as significant a part in the public relations agenda for today's leaders as they have ever done. They are consistently presented in ways that remind us of their importance, their insightfulness and their infallibility. The difference in today's less deferential world is that these images can be used to undermine the pretensions of leadership just as much as they can reinforce them.

In recent times the image and positioning of the leader as the incarnation of the state has been used to great effect, most notably in the UK where a recent report on the removal of democratic accountability of the government was presented under a cover showing Tony Blair's face superimposed on the famous portrait of Louis XIV, with the title: 'L' etat, c'est moi?'.

If art is a mirror of society[6] then what it tells us is this: whilst we may want to see changes to how leaders behave, one of the big constraints we face is that our leaders still carry the expectations set by their predecessors. We want them to know the answers, to understand our needs and aspirations, to solve our problems and to protect us from ourselves as much as from others. In fact, the model of leadership still expected and applied in the early part of the 21st century is that of parent. From renaissance princes through imperialism to the 20th century's dictators so many of history's leaders have styled themselves as 'fathers' or 'mothers' of the nation (the modern tribe). Leaders within these tribes (such as leaders in organizations) sit in organizational structures that reinforce these expectations. They are still judged by performance models that reinforce the importance of infallibility.

Malcolm Higgs[7] offers us an historical assessment of the development of the understanding of leadership taking Plato's proposition that 'society values whatever is honoured there' as his starting point. He usefully divides mankind's exploration of leadership into four historical phases: classical, renaissance, industrial and modern, recording the dominant discourse and defining each age through the eyes of the major thinkers on the nature of the leadership of the day.

This modern concept of leadership is not that promoted by Aristotle of a virtuous leader as the servant of the state, democrati-

Table 1.1 Leadership Discourses: An historical perspective

Era	Dominant Discourse	Example of Authors
Classical	Dialogue	• Plato
	Society	• Aristotle
	Democracy	• Homer
		• Pericles
		• Sophocles
Renaissance	Ambition	• Petrarch
	Individual	• Chaucer
	Great Man not Great	• Castiglione
	Event	• Machiavelli
		• Shakespeare
Industrial	Survival of the Fittest	• Weber
	Control	• Darwin
	Rationality	• Durkheim
		• Marx
Modern	Psychological	• Freud
	Behavioural	• Skinner
		• Jung

cally (however restricted the franchise) appointed and accountable to others for their leadership. Nor does it resonate fully with Machievelli's renaissance prince where coalition, alliance and the search for common ground drives achievement of ambition for the city-state. It is the direct inheritor of the concept of enlightened absolutism where the leader is firmly established as the state appointed by birth and accountable to themselves and of course God. Importantly, as they were God's appointed representative on earth they were the only person apart from the Pope – mercifully far less powerful by this time – who could articulate with assurance whatever the divine purpose was. So for all intents and purposes they were it.

Whilst birth has been replaced in political leadership – though not expunged if we consider the Kennedys in America, the Mitterands in France and the Churchills and the Pakenhams in the UK – it still plays a role in business, especially in financial services and in the media where family dynasties run their organizations with the same streak of ruthlessness as an 18th century despot. Even if the appointment process has been more open, once appointed, chief executives in public as well as private companies can and do exhibit the same characteristics and behaviour.

The global financial crisis has exposed the hubris and despotic tendencies of the leaders of many of the world's largest banks and insurance companies. Before them came the leaders of Enron, WorldCom, Parmalat and others such as Robert Maxwell, all of whom lived like kings and many of whom behaved like tyrants. Elected political leaders too, regardless of their position on the left – right spectrum, seem to have the same propensity as their counterparts in business to assume the mantle of the enlightened autocrat. In Europe most French Presidents since DeGaulle have upheld the autocratic tradition and today Italy's Silvio Berlusconi and Russia's Vladimir Putin are examples of the historical autocratic leadership traditions in their own cultures. In the UK Prime Minister Tony Blair's use of executive power has ensured his place in history as one of the most controlling leaders of government in the last 100 years.

F. W. Taylor's[8] invention of scientific management captured the essence of the industrial age by applying rationality to the organization of work and the disciplines required to manage complex production structure. What it failed to do is to give us an equally compelling explanation of leadership. Indeed despite the significant shifts in political and economic structures during the first couple of decades of the 20th century the reality of leadership has hardly changed at all. This is despite 'leadership' becoming one of the most written about topics in the world of management. Indeed as at March 2010 the only category of business and management books with a greater count on Amazon's web site was strategy (c. 230,000 vs. c. 150,000 on leadership). Perhaps even more telling is the fact that of the books listed nearly 900 were for publication over the following 15 months.[9]

This explosion in the oeuvre is the product of the application of the scientific approach to management. It reflects an increasing desire to understand why some organizations performed better than others and to apply the lessons learned elsewhere. Everyone knows that leaders matter, but the struggle is to successfully define why. At the heart of this is the belief that performance will be improved by getting leaders to adopt specific behaviours. This approach has been accelerated by the rise of the business school in which academics are encouraged to research and publish in order to satisfy both their own career ambitions and the ambitions of their employers to be regarded as 'experts' to attract government and business funding.

REPLICATING LEADERSHIP SUCCESS

This scientific approach to the understanding of effective management and leadership of organizations was accelerated by the application of social science research techniques to human interactions in organizations. Early work included that of Professor Meredith Belbin on the human contribution to effective teams. Belbin's observations of teams working on the 1960s equivalent of what is now the full time senior executive MBA programme at Henley Business School defined the combination of human attributes required for a team to be successful at achieving a task. He was not interested in changing people but rather in ensuring they were combined in such a way as to be effective.[10] His team model became the mainstay of much of the work done in organizations on improving team impact and can still be found in practice today.

In the United States, however, an approach more rooted in psychology developed from the early work of David McClelland, the American psychologist, on the motivations that underpinned achievement and predictors of job success. It aspired to create templates for successful performance in roles against which organizations could recruit, performance manage and develop their employees. This produced what is now known as the competency movement. This argued that it was possible to identify skill and behavioural traits that correlated with successful outcomes in organizations through applying empirical social science research principles to the evaluation of what successful leaders do. Having identified these competencies, proponents such as Robert Boyatzis[11] claimed that it was then possible to assess leaders and potential leaders against these criteria and to make recruitment, development and promotion decisions using these assessments. Boyatzis' model made a significant contribution to understanding what differentiated success. His critical incident based research identified nine aspects of personal performance that differentiated effective management from the less effective.[12] He identified the drivers of an individual's motivation to achieve which can be grouped into aspects of personal drive. This focused on efficiency and achievement; being active rather than passive in getting things done; self-confidence; establishing and using networks; intellectual ability (critical reasoning and synthetic thinking; diagnostic skills in using concepts and turning them into practical tools) and influencing skills (concern with own impact and use of power; effective communication oral and visual; managing group processes). Much of this work underpins leadership potential identification and development in organizations today.

This thinking gave rise to much of today's cult of the leader. As with all such outcomes the basic principles and argument are sound. To be an effective leader one has to have drive, intellectual and emotional abilities. As a model through which we can think about leadership development and appointment to leadership positions it has its utility. However, it pays no attention to the culture or environment within which a leader might be acting, and offers little or no insight into what makes, for example, for effective leadership of a group process in terms of style and approach. Nor does it argue that all of these attributes have to be present in one person for them to be fully effective.

Regardless of these caveats, competencies went into the management lexicon. They are now a standard part of recruitment and development assessments, annual performance reviews, 360 degree feedback surveys and many other activities that assail people as they attempt to carry out their activities in the modern organization. The implementation of the competency model, driven mainly by a revitalized personnel function (renaming itself along the way 'Human Resources' and adopting the pseudo-psychological jargon of the psychotherapist or life coach) resulted in it being distorted. The assessment methodology and the division of individual attributes into strengths and weaknesses built a subtly different proposition: the existence of the Mary Poppins Manager – practically perfect in every way.

Inevitably, every leader or aspiring leader looked to ensure that every area of competency was perceived by their bosses as a strength. Where a weakness was identified, for it not to be seen as a potential career roadblock, it had to be one that peers and bosses would see as 'acceptable'. Normally these are associated as a consequence of being strong in a particular area. A standard one in all the organizations I have worked in was 'not tolerating fools gladly' – a clear correlation of a consequence of high drive and a high desire to achieve. Line managers often tried to put across tougher messages using positive language to 'soften the blow'. This made it at times virtually impossible to decipher what the real issue was and whether it got in the way of effective delivery or not. Even when Human Resources changed weaknesses to 'development needs' to encourage greater openness and honesty in recording this information this same approach to the annual performance assessment round continued, after all they were still really weaknesses, weren't they? With the introduction of 360 degree feedback mechanisms some rebalancing was achieved in 'current performance' against the standards but the same basic premise still stands today: perfection is preferable.

What this proposition creates is insecurity. Leaders and potential leaders in organizations today are actively persuaded not to value themselves, their talents and abilities but to value an entirely theoretical model of perfection. This concept of a perfect leader has not existed before today in any serious consideration of leaders and leadership in society. Any brief engagement with Shakespeare, Chaucer, Machiavelli, Freud or Jung would quickly conclude that it is the imperfections of leaders that makes them so effective, just as much as those things they do well. There is no doubt in my mind that we all should learn and change at every stage of our lives. But we will all make mistakes at every stage and at every level of seniority we achieve. The challenge is to learn from these and not continue to make them. To do this is to celebrate your humanity, your imperfections and your fallibilities as well as your abilities and skills. Whilst you can be conscious of these and try to adjust your behaviour to improve your chances of success in all things, you cannot change your fundamental personality.

What makes us successful as a species is our diversity. What has brought us down in the past and will do so again in the future is conformity. The consequences of a model that suggests you can achieve perfection are potentially highly damaging for society as well as for those who submit to requirement to conform.

GURUS AND VOODOO

This requirement for perfection presented the opportunity for the rise of the leadership guru. A global market emerged in *how* to be successful as a leader as opposed to *what* an effective leader needed to do. Required to conform, we looked for those who could help us become a new person, a better person and ultimately a more successful person. At the popular end of the market we are obsessed with 'learning the secrets' from big name practitioners such as Jack Welch, through the more prosaic material of the one-minute manager to the positively ludicrous. In his book *How Mumbo Jumbo Conquered the World* polemicist and commentator Francis Wheen[13] draws our attention to the following management titles:

- 'The Leadership Secrets of Attila the Hun'
- 'Gandhi – the Heart of an executive'
- 'Confucius in the board Room'
- 'If Aristotle ran General Motors'
- 'Elizabeth I, CEO: Strategic Lessons in Leadership from the woman who built an empire'
- 'Moses CEO'
- And my favourite:'Make it so: Management Lessons from Star Trek the Next Generation'.

Wheen's analysis of what he calls 'management voodoo' exposes the fallacious nature of much of what is presented as insights into leadership success. He reminds us that much of this empty analysis – he calls it 'cracker mottoes'– comes from the (mainly) American self-help industry. The gurus that industry has created are paid tens of thousands of dollars a day to peddle these secrets of success. These have included amongst many hundreds Tom Peters, Zig Ziglar, Stephen Covey, Deepak Chopra and Anthony Robbins whose book *Giant Steps* has 365 lessons in self mastery, of which lesson 364 is this: 'Remember to expect miracles … because you are one'.[14]

This industry was, in 2006, reported as being worth about $9.6 bn in the USA alone.[15] Organizations have fallen over themselves to incorporate these insights into their management practice. Deepak Chopra's *Lessons from the Teaching of Merlin* which was so successful that it encouraged executives from computer giant 'Atlantic Richfield' to employ his company for ten years to teach employees to find their 'inner space'.[16]

These gurus have pulled off the feat of combining fireside hokey with state of the art new age management jargon. They talk about benchmarking, re-engineering, personal growth and pro-activity and in so doing have developed the standing of the village witch doctor or wise woman. Their influence on more than business and management was confirmed in the exposure of 'Wackygate' during the first Clinton administration. In the nadir of the political and personal doldrums in 1994 the Clintons invited amongst others Stephen Covey and Marianne Williamson the celebrated spiritualist and new age author to a weekend at Camp David to re-establish the vision of The Presidency. Along with this group came Jean Houston, the founder and principal teacher of 'the Mystery School', a bicoastal seminar ($2,995 per student) of 'cross-cultural, mythic and spiritual studies, dedicated to teaching history, philosophy, the New Physics, psychology, anthropology, myth and the many dimensions of human potential'. She described herself as a 'scholar, philosopher and researcher in Human Capacities'.[17] The outcome gleefully reported in the media was an apparent séance where the future presidential hopeful and Secretary of State was reported as having talked to Eleanor Roosevelt and Mahatma Gandhi who was reported as being described as a symbol of 'stoic self-denial'.[18]

Mrs Clinton is not the only leader or spouse of a leader to fall under the spell of new age management nonsense: Cherie Booth, wife of UK Prime Minister Tony Blair brought her own lifestyle guru and new age thinker, Carole Caplin, into Number 10 Downing Street to general media hilarity. Like the Clintons and the Blairs the leaders of many modern organizations have swallowed a series of increasingly preposterous propositions about leadership and management that taken together have become the tenets of faith on which the cult of the modern leader has been built. The financial crisis has finally started to expose the cult for what it is and those who follow it are today's Emperor: they are wearing no clothes.

In his seminal paper 'On Bullshit'[19] Harry G. Frankfurt points out that the essence of bullshit is not that it is false, but that it is phoney. It is unavoidable, he argues, whenever circumstances require someone to talk without knowing what he is talking about. This can be applied to much of what is written about management and leadership today. At its best it is platitudinous and unenlightening and at its worst it combines new age nonsense with the downright dangerous and dresses it up in psychobabble.

What is even more depressing is that management is full of people who seem highly susceptible to this bullshit. This can be attributed to the idea that the competency movement has created a less confident cadre in organizations today than we had thirty or forty years ago. Vulnerable and in search of an answer we instinctively turn to solutions that resonate with the certainties of our childhood. We respond with alacrity to neo-religious propositions that are delivered with all the certainty of an American evangelist preacher. We are especially impressed by anything that is presented in a way that sounds like it is based in scientific rigour.

Jamie Whyte[20] in his book, *Bad Thoughts* argues that this is the foundation for the success of management consulting in selling the simple and straightforward as complex and insightful and being able to command significantly inflated fees for so doing. He argues that, if you want to do this well, you should employ as much jargon as possible. He reminds us that there is a significant difference between jargon and terminology:

> Jargon in management consulting involves the substitution of bizarre, large and opaque words for ordinary, small and well understood words. The substitution is no more than that. Consultese brings with it no extra rigour, no measurement precision lacking in the ordinary language it replaces. Where terminology in science aids clarity and testability, consulting jargon shrouds quite plain statements in chaotic verbiage.

In the world of leadership jargon dominates. Cults thrive where there is doubt, uncertainty and anxiety. We are sold snake oil when we lack real understanding. This type of nonsense permeates management in all sectors and across all cultures.

It is this that has turned 'leadership' into a cult and as we know, cults are unhealthy. This cult sets leaders apart. It makes them special. It flatters them. It imbues them with powers over and above those of ordinary mortals. It argues that they can be spotted early, indeed that they may even be ordained from birth. This is the foundation of eighteenth century antinomianism (the belief that the elect are not subject to mortal law). And many of today's leaders have become the modern equivalent of James Hogg's justified sinner, Robert Wringham, who saw himself as 'the sword of the Lord' and when being challenged on his deadly actions justified himself as one of the great elect through 'the doctrine of grace'. On being told that even this was no justification for his action he reflects that 'the man apparently thought I was deranged in my intellect. He couldn't swallow such great truths at the first morsel.'[21] Today's versions of 'the elect' would include amongst their numbers Sir Fred Goodwin arguing that his pension arrangements were unexceptional and various members of the UK's House of Commons who seemed to feel that it was unreasonable for the public to want total transparency in the accounting for taxpayers' money spent on maintaining their second homes.

MANAGEMENT OR LEADERSHIP?

One of the reasons modern organizations have engaged with the cult is that those who lead them and especially those who lead their Human Resources functions conflate good management with leadership. A review of recent research about training needs in the UK[22] showed that many responses relating to 'leadership' were really about people management skills. The leadership skills gaps identified were:

- leading people and people management;
- leading and managing change;
- business and commercial acumen – strategic thinking;
- coaching, mentoring and developing people;
- performance management, especially standards;
- communication/interpersonal skills;
- innovation.

Whilst a couple of these include the word, none of these address the fundamentals of leadership; all are skills we require in managers at just about every level of the organization. I believe that this reflects a muddle amongst HR people specifically and the wider management population generally. It also fails to reflect the increasing need in the new world to ensure that as leaders we understand the business we are in. One of the significant criticisms of the big banks is that many of their leaders were responsible for organizations selling products they as leaders did not understand; hence the call for a return to appointing leaders who understand what it takes to be good at banking.

Leadership is somehow a 'bigger and better' version of management: something strategic and somehow more critical than just managing people. Attending a leadership programme has far more kudos than attending one on management. Certainly this is backed up by my experience in business education where there is evidence to show that changing the title of a product to incorporate 'leadership' as a training provider results in your selling more places. It flatters the attendee and in a world where words like 'executive', 'director' and 'senior' are used to such a degree that they are significantly devalued against their original meaning, attending a mere management programme suggests a very lowly level of career attainment.

If there is one emerging differentiator between the challenges of leadership and those of management it is that associated with globalization. This is likely to be the century where, regardless of the views of the political classes, borders will come down. As they recede what will appear is both a more connected yet more fragmented world. It is more connected, thanks to the rise of technology, the breaking down of barriers to travel and the ubiquity of brands that address basic human needs regardless of culture.

It is a more fragmented world, in that the wider the common interest group we belong to, the more likely we are to look for local connection, for roots and for personal differentiation. This is the driver behind the rise of nationalism across Europe from Scotland to Serbia. This too plays to a basic human need: that of belonging and acceptance. It will be increasingly difficult to manage cross-border organizations in this world unless leaders from all walks of life take on some of the bigger issues facing humanity regardless of where they live and what they do. The more complex and ambiguous our world becomes so much greater becomes the need for immediate certainty and community. This is the paradox that has to be resolved by the leaders of modern organizations. We now have to understand power and how to make this power work positively for people in a far more integrated, connected, yet at the same time fragmented and conflicted world. What leadership thinking has to embrace is the role of power and how it is distributed, looking for models that reflect the ambiguity within which we live: decentralizing that which we need to run our day-to-day lives, and pooling that which we need to resolve the significant cross-border challenges that we face. In this regard, power itself indeed is not the issue, the issue is how those with power exercise it and what we as citizens perceive as the outcomes of the use of that power. For those of us who believe that the creation of wealth and the use of it to better humanity in a sustainable way should be the foundation on which the exercise of power should be built, are looking for leadership we can trust.

The study of human and organization behaviour is not about the discovery of the new. Rather, it is about explaining better what we can all see, which in turn opens up new possibilities for the re-shaping and transformation of our social environment. Today's leaders in a globalizing world must understand that those issues central to leadership: motivation, inspiration, sensitivity and communication have changed little in 3,000 years. There is nothing to suggest that the process of globalization itself will change this one iota. What it does is make it far more challenging.

WHAT LEADERS DO WRONG

Early on in this chapter I referred to work done by my colleague Professor Malcolm Higgs and in his latest work[23] he addresses the darker side of leadership. His research reinforces what we know to be the habits of many modern leaders:

(i) Abuse of power. This encompasses the abuse of power to serve personal goals or achieve personal gain; the use of power to reinforce self-image and enhance perceptions of personal performance; and the abuse of power to conceal personal inadequacies.

(ii) Inflicting damage on others. This focuses on negative impact on subordinates and includes: bullying; coercion; negative impact on perceptions of subordinate self-efficacy; damage to the psychological well-being of subordinates; and inconsistent or arbitrary treatment of subordinates.

(iii) Over-exercise of control to satisfy personal needs. For example: obsession with detail; perfectionism and limiting subordinate initiative.

(iv) Rule breaking to serve own purposes. This is the area of behaviour in which leaders engage in corrupt, unethical and, indeed, illegal behaviour.

(v) The ability of leaders to engage in 'bad' behaviour is seen to emanate from their positional power.

Let me give you one story of many that exist in business of these behaviours coming together to act in a way guaranteed to undermine confidence in the leaders of business. In their book *The New Capitalists* the authors claim that in the public merger negotiations with WorldCom in 2,000, executives in the telecom firm Sprint borrowed millions of dollars to exercise their stock options and purchase stock which they believed would continue to increase in value. This created a significant tax obligation. When the merger discussions fell apart the share price more than halved slashing their personal gains but not their tax liabilities.

Accountants Ernst & Young provided both tax advice and audit services to Sprint and to support the executives from whom they earned their fees they advised that Sprint could repossess the options saving the executives concerned, including the CEO, more than $300 million in paper profits and thereby remove their tax liabilities. This move would have cost the company's shareowners $148 million in tax benefits. Sprint eventually decided not to implement the plan but the fact they gave it consideration and that their advisors were asked to work on it demonstrates how divorced senior leaders can become from the realities of what the rest of us believe is right and wrong.[24]

Ernst & Young are currently facing questions about their role in the auditing of Lehman Brothers' accounts in the year prior to the collapse of the bank. The role of advisers, often retained to give confidence to the owners of the business that the rules are being followed and that executives are acting in the owners' best interests, is increasingly coming under the microscope as disgruntled owners challenge the behaviour of executives.

There is no doubt that behaviour like this can only destroy wealth, value and economic performance. Many sit at the heart of what happened in big business and in regulatory authorities during the last ten years. It is now time to accept imperfection, fallibility and humanity; to expect less of one person and more of a team; in other words to reposition the leadership model in the realities of the new world.

WHY WE NEED LEADERSHIP

We have to address some very awkward questions about leadership. Perhaps whilst we still live in tribes there is a limitation to the development of leadership? Maybe we crave the security of knowing someone else is taking care of things? Maybe most of us are reluctant to take responsibility and are only too happy for others to step up? Is it better to be able to blame someone else when something goes wrong rather than accept responsibility for ourselves? Social psychologists have conducted numerous studies that demonstrate that human beings have a significant dread of making the wrong decisions. In one particular study it was shown that people avoid choices between very similar options by postponing them or through other equally effective strategies for procrastination including persuading themselves that there is no need to make a choice at all.[25]

Heroic leadership is the life-blood of Hollywood and the core of many school history books. But it is rarely the reality, and even when it is it can only be so for a short period of time when our community, our tribe or our society, is threatened with overwhelming danger. In leadership you can make a difference or no difference. This is well illustrated in a comparison made between John F. Kennedy's Peace Corps and Newt Gingrich's 'Contract with America'. The former, still going strong after fifty years, is based in the leadership proposition that it was better to 'ask what you could do for your country' whilst the latter lasted a single term based as it was on the message 'Vote for us, then sit back and watch us perform. We'll take care of it for you.'[26] Having failed to take care of it Gingrich and his colleagues were voted out. This illustration comes from Roger Martin's book exploring the difficulty of establishing personal responsibility in organizations. Martin's argument gives insight to the importance of leadership over that of one heroic leader. Hegel argued that human beings have within them a pre-established 'master-slave dialect', in other words that a partnership of equals was a rarity and the normal state of affairs was for one human being to dominate another. This drives a tendency in humans to flip from dominance to subservience depending on the relationship we are experiencing at any one time. Martin builds on this and suggests that we are all driven by a fear of failure and we react in one of two ways: take more responsibility than we need to or should (i.e. dominate and become the heroic leader) or take less (i.e. to stand back and await instructions from others, refusing to take on responsibility where we could and should). The challenge for leaders is not to do the former and to ensure those you lead do not do the latter.

There is something in modern society, however, that conspires against that very rational proposition. In a world far more democratic and open than the one in which Hegel developed his ideas, people are often less willing than their predecessors to stand up and take responsibility either for resolving problems in their organizations, their communities or even their families, or for the consequences of their actions. We are far too willing to blame others and far less willing to accept our own role or contribution. We expect those in leadership positions to have all the answers and to fix all the problems and we then criticize them at the first sign of doubt or failure. We don't need these sorts of leaders: their failure is inevitable as those they lead are unwilling to work with them to find solutions and to play their role in making change happen. We need leadership. We need all of us to take the lead, to act in line with the common purpose of our organizations. To achieve this we will need to promote the adoption of values far more akin to those of John F. Kennedy's vision of America than those that have dominated in the last twenty years of the 20th century.

Chapter Two
Because We're Worth It
The Rise of the L'Oreal Generation

The story of the failure of leadership in modern organizations is the story of what one might call the 'L'Oreal generation.'[1] This was the generation that was owed a living; career success; a house that doubled in value every 5–10 years; a new car on the drive every other year; the latest technology; the quickest broadband; and a body that no longer showed signs of age. This was the generation that believed it could cheat death itself. They were owed these things because they were worth it. They hadn't worked as hard for it, hadn't saved for it, hadn't forgone things to afford it and they certainly hadn't thought through whether they really needed it. It was there. Everyone else had it, so why shouldn't they? Their sense of self-worth was sufficient. Indeed, they were worth less in the eyes of others if they didn't have all the trappings of success so they went about looking for the funds to acquire the body, the clothes, the living space, the hobbies and the holidays that told the world they were the chosen ones. As a result they have ended up defining their self-worth through the continual acquisition and consumption of things.

This generation is the product of a significant shift in values in society. At the end of the Second World War the defining value set in the United Kingdom could be described as both strongly homogeneous and centred on the importance of society as a whole. People accepted the need to give up things that were important to them such that the country could recover from the ravages of war. There was a corporatist perspective in how people thought about social problems and this supported a belief that there was a role for the state in providing benefits and support and in leading the development of the economy for the benefit of all. This was the generation of the national health service, the expansion of education, the nationalization of rail transport, fuel and steel production and of thrift.

Reporting from the British Values Survey which has tracked attitudes in the UK since the end of the Second World War shows just how marked the shift away from this clear homogenous world view was in the 1970s, 1980s and 1990s towards individualism and self-centeredness. Not just this but how much more heterogeneous values are across the population. In the 1980s and 1990s the country increasingly divided into different value sets (reflecting the impacts of immigration, of education and of a more liberal social attitudes in society itself) with the old values still held to dearly by one section of the population and the new values equally strongly embraced by another. These new values themselves are conflicting with a strong individualist self-centred and socially and economically ambitious group sharing the country with a more externally focused, socially aware group whose values could be defined as broadly 'liberal' or 'progressive' and whose concerns would be more internationalist and environmental than for achieving maximum financial rewards. This split in values can be seen in a more polarized media, in strong differences in voting patterns and in widely differing attitudes to issues such as debt. The part of this new generation that were driven by individual achievement and personal rewards for success became the role models for organizational success.

Much of this new generation, unlike the generation that shaped the UK after the Second World War, do not define themselves by their political or economic convictions. In a report on the possible outcomes of the 2010 general election in the UK it was reported that only one in eight of the UK's population claims that their political convictions make up any part of their self identity. Seven out of eight of the British population does not feel that politics has any relevance to their self identity. The authors go on to say:

> To put this into some sort of context, almost 19%, close to one in five, chose 'my body, face, and hair' as a self identifier. An ad for L'Oreal 'Because You're Worth It' is more likely to make a connection with self identity than any politically slanted ad.[2]

This is the generation that has found its way into power. In politics, in business and in the media you can see these people today. They revel in self-promotion, in display and in the trappings of success. They too have spawned an even more extreme group in the population. In an addendum to a report produced for IPPR on consumer power in 2009 researchers introduced the concept of 'Now People'. These are the shock troops of the L'Oreal generation. They direct all of their energy and social skills to identify and acquire the symbols that can establish themselves as the central players in networks that they themselves establish and maintain for the sole reason of reinforcing the importance to their lives of the symbols they have acquired.[3] This is the group that provides contestants for 'The Apprentice' and 'Big Brother'.

This shift in values can be tracked in popular culture with the introduction into common usage of the concept of a 'lifestyle' and the word surfaces some time in the last twenty-five years of the 20th century to become common parlance used to describe the way in which we live or want to live by the early 1990s.[4] The *Oxford Dictionary of Current English* offers this definition from 2006:

> the way in which a person or group lives: the benefits of a healthy lifestyle. [as adj.] denoting advertising or products designed to appeal to a consumer by association with a desirable lifestyle.[5]

As the 21st century began we were living in the world of the makeover: your house, your clothes, your body, could all be changed to suit the 'lifestyle' you had chosen for yourself. This was the consummation of consumption capability as the apotheosis of the consumer society. It was the only path through which happiness could be obtained. A path that as the century dawned has become one of the most important drivers of human behaviour not just in the Western world but for many in the developing economies of the Middle East and Asia.

We no longer have a life. We no longer make a living. Now we have to have a lifestyle. In this lifestyle we no longer learn and change as a result of learning but we go on a journey. Advertising and promotions create pictures of the 'lifestyles' to which we are encouraged to aspire and the people we will become if only we had the mobile, the clothes, the car and the age-removing cosmetic adjustment, surgical or chemical. For the aspiring corporate executive, an essential part of the lifestyle was to be seen to be regarded by your employer as 'talent'. Success was no longer the German company car on the drive, the two foreign holidays a year or even the timeshare in Florida; to be able to portray yourself as successful you had to be clearly identifiable as 'top talent'.

Prior to the global financial crisis, one of the biggest drivers of activity in major corporations was a focus on the 'war for talent'. The obsession with identifying, retaining – often at any cost – and focusing your development investment on 'talented people' was already seen as corrosive at the turn of the century. Malcolm Gladwell[6] writing in *The New Yorker* in 2002 argued that this, more than anything else in modern organizations, was responsible for undermining corporations and their ability to do the right things right. He defined his proposition very clearly:

> This 'talent mind-set' is the new orthodoxy of American man-
> agement. It is the intellectual justification for why such a high
> premium is placed on degrees from first-tier business schools,
> and why the compensation packages for top executives have
> become so lavish. In the modern corporation, the system is
> considered only as strong as its stars, and, in the past few
> years, this message has been preached by consultants and
> management gurus all over the world.

Gladwell aimed his biggest kick at McKinsey & Co as the pro-moters and champions of this talent-led philosophy. He linked their ideas to Enron, who put them into practice with a vengeance, hiring at one stage over 250 of the smartest MBAs in America in a year and, to quote one of their directors, 'paying them more than they think they are worth'. Yet there is no correlation in any reputable research between IQ and success in a job. This demolition of the consulting model of talent recruitment and development which had invaded Wall Street and The City and was already distorting reward strategies and senior management behaviour should have rung alarm bells in boardrooms all over the world. The fact it didn't, despite the considerable publicity it got at the time shows just how far this thinking had become management orthodoxy amongst the leaders of so much of the world's financial services sector.

The critics of the 'War for Talent' theory argue that its acceptance and implementation creates a 'Narcissistic Organization': one that is led and peopled by individuals who are reinforced in their self-belief every day by systems of reward and promotion that confirm their abilities. This concept is one that fits so many of the collapsed and near-collapsed companies in the financial services sector. Gladwell cites a definition from Hogan, Raskin and Fazzini in their essay entitled 'The Dark Side of Charisma':[7]

> Narcissists typically make judgments with greater confidence than other people ... and, because their judgments are rendered with such conviction, other people tend to believe them and the narcissists become disproportionately more influential in group situations. Finally, because of their self-confidence and strong need for recognition, narcissists tend to 'self-nominate'; consequently, when a leadership gap appears in a group or organization, the narcissists rush to fill it.

Enron is one of the best and most well-known examples of the Narcissistic Corporation: a company so clever at self-promotion that it became the darling of business schools and business academics as well as Wall Street. Its successes were trumpeted way beyond what they were really worth and were cleverly used by an organization able to sell analysts and academics alike on its genius. In other words it substituted self-nomination for disciplined management. A great example of the effect of 'the sell' to business school gurus was the way Enron became one of the big cases in showing how innovation can drive business performance used by top business school guru Dr Gary Hamel, in his work in the 1990s. A post-scandal Hamel in the introduction to his book *Leading the Revolution*[8] argues that Enron's mistake was applying the same creativity they used in business to their balance sheet and that, combined with rushing 'pell-mell over the line that separates ambition from hubris' was where they went wrong. Fooling even the best thinkers in the world, Enron was able to use all the charms and wiles of a narcissist to sell itself as the opportunity for 1990s investors looking to get rich quick.

Human frailties and fallibilities are nothing new and are accountable for much in history. The attraction of opportunities to get rich quick provided through speculative behaviour litters economic history books. Tulipomania in the Netherlands (1634–1637) is one of the earliest examples of a fashion that saw investors flock into a perceived opportunity to make a fortune only for it to end in ruin. Imported from the Middle East to decorate the homes of the wealthy, by the early 1630s the tulip had established itself as a highly desirable flower. Ownership and display of tulips became the 17th century's equivalent of the yuppie symbol of success in the 1980s: a BMW on the drive. Prices were so high that people left their jobs, sold their houses, cashed in their valuables and started to buy up tulips. They were traded in exchanges and became a currency in themselves. The fall in prices came suddenly with a loss of confidence and ultimately destroyed the livelihoods of thousands of people. The economic depression that followed was lengthy.[9] The Missouri Madness in France (1717–1720) was the consequence of a plan by Scottish financier, John Law, backed by the government of the Regent, Philip, Duke of Orleans. The plan was to fund an expansion in credit through gathering the monopoly of trade with Louisiana (the Mississippi Company) and the farming of the taxes into one organization that then took control of the royal debt. The consequent speculation in the value of the bank's shares and the crash that followed had significant economic consequences.[10] In the UK, the South Sea Bubble development in the UK charted a similar course to that of the Missouri Madness in France at roughly the same time. John Law's scheme was seen as something investors wished to replicate in London. Again, the company aimed at exploiting a monopoly of trade, this time with the South Seas. It took over a significant proportion of government debt in exchange for being able to issue stock to the same value. Outbidding the Bank of England (still a private bank) for the rights to own the debt, much in the manner of Law's French company outbidding the Farmers-General for the right to manage the collection of taxation, the South Sea Company then applied sophisticated financial engineering to keep the price of their stock increasing to what were unimaginable heights. The crash came as the engineering collapsed and it took the 18th century equivalent of the recent state bail-out of the banks to steady The City and to ensure that economic prospects were protected.[11] Whilst this and the Missouri Madness in France bear striking similarities to the rise of global financial markets in the 1990s and the 2000s,

Tulipomana has more in common with the much more recent 'dot
-com' bubble of the 1990s. However, what they demonstrate ably
is that those with the resources to invest have always looked for the
opportunity to move ahead of the market and to get out at the top.
For the few winners in a bubble there were many more losers whose
often hard-earned cash was lost and quite often such losses ended
up in ruin, and imprisonment for debt (until debt was decriminal-
ized) or worse.

What differentiates the most recent crisis from these others,
including even the 'dot-com' bubble, is the combination of the globalization of business and the capital markets from which business
gets its investment finance and the deregulation of financial services in key markets (especially those in the Anglo-Saxon tradition).
This has changed three things about speculation. First, the creation
of investment vehicles that pool capital from large groups of small
investors (these range from bank depositors, through insurance
and pension fund members to direct investment funds in capital
markets) gave huge power and influence to a few investment fund
managers to drive market behaviour. Secondly, the availability of
significant levels of low-cost liquidity that could be rapidly transferred around the globe gave access to capital to people willing to
take significantly higher risk profiles which created hedge funds,
arbitrage houses and the like whose influence on the system has
become considerable. Thirdly, the level of the sums involved and
the link that this has to the ultimate reward for fund managers and
their bosses in financial services.

These changes have transformed capital markets, banking
and related financial services and the market for organization
leaders across all sectors of the economy. Capital markets where

speculation drives a significant slice of the action become far shorter-term in their assessment of the value of an investment and far more interested in capital growth than regular income generation. They become less interested in the long-term success of the enterprise and much more exercised in a narrower concept of shareholder value associated purely with financial returns. This drives market behaviour that looks both ways and starts to take bets on failure as well as success.

This is well illustrated by the Porsche/Volkswagen debacle of 2008 where speculation drove an outcome that valued a struggling European carmaker higher than Exxon-Mobil, the world's largest oil company, making it briefly the world's most valuable company. This episode exposed to greater public awareness the impact of two practices increasingly adopted in the market by traders more interested in generating significant bonuses than in the real value of the investment opportunity with which they were being presented: short selling (or shorting) and stock loaning. The general sentiment in the world's financial markets in 2008 was that car producers were unlikely to perform well in the foreseeable future given the state of the world's economy and the link between economic growth and car sales. In these circumstances speculative funds such as hedge funds look to take a bet on the market that shares in specific companies would fall. They operate a system whereby they sell assets at a higher price looking to buy them back at a lower price in the future. Speculators don't often own stock in these circumstances but use the opportunity to 'borrow' it from longer-term owners such as institutional investors. Stock gets borrowed at a set price and is returned within an agreed period. Institutional investors gain through the fee for the 'loan' and the speculator makes their profit on the difference between the selling price and the buy-back price handing back the same shares, now worth considerably less.

In Germany Volkswagen (VW) was identified as a certain loser from the decline in car sales globally and a considerable amount of stock was 'shorted'. Unknown to the hedge funds, the carmaker Porsche had been buying up VW stock, aiming to secure the majority of the company. When this became clear the market reacted by pushing VW stock higher, rather than lower as the speculators had gambled. As the price rose it made VW one of the biggest companies on the German market and as a result drew in institutional investors such as pension funds who just pushed the price even higher. The consequence was a major failure of confidence in the German market and a series of legal cases alleging fraud as many of the world's speculative funds made serious losses.[12] Another century: another bubble.

With financial deregulation banking and investment houses moved into each others' territories, merged, acquired and bought up capabilities, often at great cost. This created giant organizations which speculated at one end, often with billions of pounds of depositors' money, and took ever increasing risks fuelled by the availability of cheap liquidity in the global wholesale markets. They often drove their retail businesses by accepting far greater risks in loans, especially those associated with property. The size of the banks, the impact of the growth in earnings on the ability of senior executives to generate serious wealth and the subsequent shifts in market rates and remuneration practice across not just financial services but into business and more recently into the public sector in some countries have been extraordinary.

The impact on business has been to create a class of senior executive that believes their talent is worth more than the capital invested in the business by shareholders. These people have taken advantage of their position, and the influence of the small coterie of fund managers, themselves highly rewarded. They have engineered a coup d'etat in which the rights of the owners of the enterprise to the lion's share of excess profits unwanted for further investment has been usurped. This cash is taken as a cost above the line and allocated to outrageous levels of personal reward, normally through bonus and share option schemes. This is the triumph of the L'Oreal generation: a narcissistic cadre of super rich individuals last seen in the developed world in the 18th and 19th centuries. A class of super-rich the vast majority of whom even fail to have the saving grace of their predecessors to understand their debt to the rest of society which has made them rich by ploughing back some of their wealth for the greater good.

Today the remuneration arguments are well rehearsed in many places. There is a plethora of statistics to show the unequal rate of growth of CEO and leadership rewards versus that of the average wage-earner and that this is not just an issue for the United States and the United Kingdom. For example in Canada in 1998, the best-paid 100 CEOs pocketed an average $3,457,150. By 2006 their average earnings increased by 146%. By contrast, the average of weekly wages and salaries increased by only 18% during that period. [13] There are many example of significant acceleration in the US and the UK. In 2006 the chief executives of America's 500 biggest companies got a collective 38% pay raise to $7.5 billion. That was an average $15.2 million apiece.[14] In the UK in 2007

Incomes Data Services, an independent research organization providing information and analysis on pay, conditions, pensions, employment law and personnel policy and practice, reported that chief executives earned on average ninety-eight times more than the average for all UK full-time workers. The interesting part is that ten years ago the pay differential was thirty-nine times that of the average worker.[15]

There has also been a significant shift in the value of the annual salary as part of the total compensation received by a senior executive as compared to share options where an individual is granted rights to access shares in the organization at an agreed price on the achievement of agreed goals. The assumption in this scheme being that if the goals are achieved the actual price of the shares would have increased, so offering a senior executive a financial gain. In 1992, executive salaries in the UK accounted for approximately 37% of total pay and share options a relatively modest 22%. As the decade wore on, options became the single most important pay element while salaries declined in importance. Now, salaries account for only about one fifth of total pay compared to share options which account for one third – the single largest element. Share options have been particularly responsible for some of the significant shifts in relative values and they are discussed in more detail in Chapter Seven.[16] Overall, share option grants comprise a much larger percentage of total pay for the average US CEO (36%) than for the average UK CEOs (10%). Compared to other countries, CEOs in the UK and US receive a relatively high proportion of their compensation in the form of options.[17] One final point on compensation: performance doesn't seem to come into it. Sixty companies at the bottom of the Russell 3000 Index in the US lost

$769 billion in market value in the five years ending 2004 while their boards paid their top five executives at each firm more than $12 billion.[18]

As I said, this is not just a UK/US issue. A study in 2008 looking at rates of pay (as oppose to total reward package values) by the Economic Policy Institute in the US, whilst it shows the particularly dramatic acceleration of CEO rates of pay in the US and the UK compared to other 'developed' economies, it also shows that across the board with one notable exception, Japan, there has been a significant growth in CEO rewards.

In particular the study looked not just at percentage growth over the period 1988–2005 in a selection of key economies within the OECD but also at two other ratios: the relationship between average CEO and manufacturing production worker pay in the United States to that received by CEOs and workers in non-US economies and the ratio in each economy between the average CEO and the average worker. The biggest increases in CEO pay over the period were in Sweden (304%), Australia (292%), Italy (232%), France (197%), Germany (187%) and Switzerland (172%). This would make the United Kingdom (161%) and United States (169%) seem relatively unexceptional until one realizes that the driver of these much higher increases was the impact of the sheer scale of CEO pay in these latter two economies. In US dollar terms the highest pay levels are US CEOs whose 2005 average earnings were $2.2 million. The highest five after this were Switzerland $1.4 million, France, Germany and the UK on $1.2 million and Italy on $1.15 million. Broadly speaking, US CEOs get about double their counterparts in other advanced economies and the relative position in every economy bar the UK and Switzerland would have been far worse had not their CEOs had such significant increases in their pay.

As far as the pay ratio between the average production worker and their CEOs are concerned, this study only looked at rates of pay rather than total earnings and when these are included the ratio between CEOs and production workers turns into multiples of one hundred; however even at the level of pay alone the ratios across these advanced economies are significant and those in the US and the UK are even more so. Excluding these two countries the average ratio in 2005 was just under twenty times more for a CEO than for a production worker. In the US it was thirty-nine times and in the UK just about thirty-two times. In only one country was it less than fifteen times: Japan, where the ratio is ten.

In the period from 1988 to 2005 corporations across the world's major developed economies, with the exception of Japan, rewarded their top managers with increases that on average saw their pay rise from anywhere between slightly under 100% to slightly over 300%. For the L'Oreal generation it reinforced just how much they were worth it.

This reinforcement of personal worth within a corporation displaying all the signs of being narcissistic is a recipe for tragedy. The hubris of Enron has been seen across many other organizations, and the global financial crisis has exposed many of them. In his follow-up novel to *Catch 22*, *Something Happened*, Joseph Heller presented a highly critical account of business life in the insurance industry in which he wrote:

Success and failure are both difficult to endure. Along with success come drugs, divorce, fornication, bullying, travel, meditation, medication, depression, neurosis and suicide. With failure comes failure.[19]

As we think about the last decade we have to ask how much did this explosion of monetary value, placed on so few individuals, reinforce their self-belief and conviction of invincibility and as a result sow the seeds of failure? What drives executives to endorse accounting practices that ultimately bankrupt not only themselves and their associates but also thousands of suppliers and investors? What drives executives to confuse their own assets with those belonging to their corporation and use the latter to fund what today's press refer to as a 'playboy lifestyle'? What drives executives to agree to mis-reporting of a major balance sheet asset and as a result lose not just their jobs but also their professional reputations? And what drives fund managers to sell non-existent investment funds to the wealthy such that they can maintain the lifestyle of their clients to such an extent that they bankrupt not just themselves but also thousands of others?

Heller's curse of success is not confined to business alone. We watch people self-destruct with unerring regularity, especially in the world of arts and entertainment where genuinely talented people can destroy themselves with the consequences of fame and celebrity. What the rise of the narcissistic manager into leadership roles has done, however, is given them the whole corporation, not just their own resources, with which to pursue their own interests. As these become increasingly out of kilter with those of the organization, the organization itself suffers. Indeed they can at their most extreme destroy the corporation itself. There is a belief that these 'dark side' characteristics are a reflection of selfishness and the degree to which, as senior executives, such people are given so much discretion by the owners of businesses that they can end up destroying large amounts of value before they are brought under control (normally at this stage, by being asked to leave).[20] Is there a potential single factor that may be common to all these circumstances? I suggest there is a link between the choices that they and many others have made. Whilst it is always difficult to speculate on individual motivation for making unacceptable choices, one thing stands out as having changed in major corporations in the last thirty years: the structure and size of the financial rewards available to top executives compared to those of the average employee.

Whilst the continued growth in the disparity of reward must be of genuine concern to shareowners and other stakeholders in society I have no problem with paying people market rates, nor with giving incentives to people to perform. I led a business school which firmly believes that the market is the only solution for allocating resources within which people can achieve personal goals and personal freedom. However, we have always put around this belief a powerful caveat: that if you build management capability to create wealth then you are creating that wealth for society as a whole. Whilst this includes wealth for the individual, there has to be an acceptance of the value of 'the greater good' otherwise the consequences are economic and social instability. What the global banking sector remuneration stories demonstrate is that if the value at stake of the incentive is so significant and the ability to influence the outcome in your favour is in your control, then the temptation to make a choice where self-interest triumphs over the interests of owners, employees, suppliers and customers is a very real one.

In this environment, leadership choices, more than any other, must take account of the widest possible interest, not just their own. In building the reputation that is so important for any organization to succeed their choices must take account of the longer-term as well as short-term perspectives. After all, leadership in the wealth-creating sector is a major responsibility. We trust these leaders to make the right choices not just for themselves or just for their organizations but also for the wider community.

This proposition is not necessarily a modern one. It resonates with Aristotle's 'good men' and has attracted many proponents; it reaches back into the emergence of the major religions; it finds itself famously represented by J. S. Mill in his articulation of the 'greater good'. However, it is in Hegel and his exploration of the drive for freedom, of 'passions' that can corrupt 'the true idea' (the right thing to do) and the susceptibility of man to both good and evil that we find the dilemma that faces all writers on leadership:[21]

No man is a hero to his valet-de-chambre but not because the former is a hero, but because the latter is a valet. ... [the leader] is devoted to the one aim regardless of all else ... so mighty a form must trample down many an innocent flower – crush to pieces many an object in its path. It is not the general idea that is implicated in opposition and combat and that is exposed to danger. It remains in the background, untouched and uninjured. This may be called the cunning of reason – that it sets the passions to work for itself, while that which develops its existence through such impulsion pays the penalty and suffers loss. ... The particular is for the most part too trifling values as compared with the general: individuals are sacrificed and abandoned. The idea pays the penalty of determinate existence and of corruptibility, not from itself, but from the passions of individuals ... individuals, to the extent of their freedom, are responsible for the depravation and enfeeblement of morals and religion. This is the seal of the absolute and sublime destiny of man – that he knows what is good and what is evil ...

There are two points here. First, that in pursuit of a worthy goal, less than worthy actions are taken by those given the power to achieve it. There would be many modern parallels with the actions of leaders today, a good example being the selective use of intelligence data by UK Prime Minister Tony Blair to justify invading Iraq and ridding the world of an appallingly brutal regime. We can all recognize this and can probably relate such stories about leadership in organizations. This is one of the challenges of leadership and one that continues to undermine leaders who forget that ultimately they lead through the acquiescence of those who follow. Keeping one's integrity intact in your dealings with individuals whilst keeping the goal in focus is a constant dilemma. Lord Acton had a point when he famously wrote 'Power tends to corrupt and absolute power corrupts absolutely'.[22] For the L'Oreal generation the opportunity to use power to acquire the symbols through which they wanted to define themselves was just too tempting and those who were able to establish absolute power were able to acquire fabulous wealth, were lionized and became celebrities. They got what they wanted.

The second point is, I think, more problematic for those of us living in the West in the second decade of the 21st century: his assumption that we know and understand what is good and what is evil. This has sat at the heart of the judicial system, of interpersonal relationships and of commerce for at least four millennia. Regardless of what we do, we are still clear on what is right and what is wrong. What we are seeing in the West over the last thirty years, however, is the dissolving of the fundamental assumption that underpinned Hegel's argument: a coherent and homogenous set of core values in a society on which a common and consistent moral and ethical understanding was based. There may be a parallel here with the rapid decline in religious belief since the end of the Second World War but whatever the cause the outcome is clear: those who do wrong in the eyes of some now feel able to walk tall in society, it would seem with no shame or regret. The appointment of the apparently disgraced former chief executive of the Royal Bank of Scotland, Sir Fred Goodwin, to a highly paid, high profile advisory role in business is one of many recent examples.

It is this much greater variety of values and the consequent disaggregation of a common view of right and wrong which has supported the justification for the continuation of excessive personal gain in the banking sector even after the traumas that immediately followed the global financial crisis. Many commentators, politicians and others have been shocked by the continued insistence of many senior executives in the sector of the importance of maintaining the remuneration principles established before the crash. The leaders of that sector continue to press their case arguing that they are forced to continue the excessive levels of compensation in the sector because they need to attract and retain their top talent. They fail to see that their position reflects a very different value system from the values held by the mainstream of society in the UK, Continental Europe and the US. Rewards, driven in the main part by bonuses, continue at levels where the take from the owners of the company is still considerably more than it was thirty years ago. Bankers justify their size and dominance as 'beneficial' for society, despite nearly having bankrupted half of the Western world. Companies continue with their persistence that only a very small number of people could do the top job and put together pay packages that reflect pre-crisis thinking.[23] The L'Oreal generation's desires and demands are more persistent than many of us had credited.

Corporate leaders have learned very little it seems from the last few years. Increasingly, they face owner push back over remuneration plans and principles. In the UK and the US even institutional shareowners are beginning to baulk at the sheer chutzpah of some of the leaders of industry. In the US discussions are underway about adopting the UK's system of advisory shareowner votes on a separate remuneration report. The UK's advisory voting process has forced some changes in practice but after the crisis questions are now being raised again about whether owners should have a mandatory role. The UK's parliamentary committee on treasury matters reported:

> Shareholders have had an advisory vote on companies' remuneration reports since 2002. However, our evidence suggests that this advisory vote has largely failed to promote enhanced scrutiny of, or provided an effective check on, remuneration policies within the sector. We believe the time is now ripe for a review of how institutional investors with holdings in the financial services sector have exercised these rights. We expect the Walker Review on corporate governance in the banking sector to examine this issue as part of its work.[24]

In 2010 major UK companies such as Marks and Spencer, J Sainsbury and Tesco all suffered significant shareowner push back on remuneration for their top executives, despite their relative success. What these votes reveal most of all is the difference in values between the real owners of the capital and fund managers who often exercise voting control due to the agglomerated value of their fund holding stake. Fund managers, often on similar schemes and levels themselves, focus far more on performance rather than actual rewards: if the company delivers they will be far less likely to object, arguing with some justification that they are not there to worry about the increasing differential relativities. Whilst this may have some justification it is short-sighted and can only drive a public reaction that could ultimately damage the whole of the wealth creating sector. The leader of the UK's Confederation of British Industry, the representative body for larger businesses, is quoted as saying:

> If leaders of big firms seem to occupy a different galaxy, they risk being treated as aliens. It is difficult to persuade the public that profits are no more than the necessary lifeblood of a successful business if they see a small cohort at the top reaping such large rewards.[25]

The L'Oreal generation is one defined by its attitude to risk. It would seem that they believe that they just can't fail. Take the acquisition of the world's largest confectionery company, Cadbury, by US conglomerate, Kraft. This has resulted in Kraft shareholders being encumbered with over $11 billion of debt without being asked for their approval and newly acquired confectionery brands with the challenge of saving approximately $700 million a year in operating costs within three years. Kraft's largest shareholder, Warren Buffet, has publicly opposed this decision.[26] As the vast majority of such acquisitions destroy shareowner value[27] one has to ponder why, given all that has happened in the corporate world, the leaders of Kraft have persuaded themselves to take such a risk with others people's money. One thing is clear: the price for failure, however spectacular and however damaging to shareowners, is no longer dismissal. It is a negotiated settlement with significant compensation and protection of valuable accrued rights such as pension entitlement. With so little of real personal value at stake could it be that senior executives are more willing to accept greater levels of risk than they did in previous generations?

This is a generation sustained by the belief that there was merit in instant gratification and self-aggrandizement. As this generation rose to the top of corporations they took the opportunity presented by deregulation and the relaxation of controls, social and legal, and executed a spectacular coup d'état against the owners of businesses. Their values and the associated standards of behaviour, however, were only one part of the problem. The changes to the shape and structure of capital ownership, the development of global financial services and the conflation of two very different types of capital structures, the limited liability corporation and the unlimited liability partnership, gave the L'Oreal generation their opportunity.

Chapter Three
Why Didn't We See It Coming?
The Loss of Liability, Stewardship and Owner Control

The Judaeo-Christian and Islamic inheritances both tell the story of Job and grant him significant status as a man whose faith supported him through a series of privations imposed on him by God. As these privations worsen, so he is comforted by those whose words only aggravated his distress. Today we, the small shareholders and pension fund members, the voters and users of public services, the saviours of the banking sector and the only source of cash for governments struggling to reduce their spending habits are the equivalent of Job.

Since the global financial crisis we have had to sit by and see our capital assets decline, our investment income reduce, our salaries (if we are in work) lose their real value and our working lives extend as the value of our pension provision shrinks. We do so regaled by pundits, thinkers, campaigners and legislators all analysing where it all went wrong, all pointing out the failures in leadership in politics, in business and in regulation none of whom can do more than make what is difficult to bear even more unbearable. The analysis on its own will not change a thing. Intellectually leaders in business may understand the problem and why their wider stakeholders are not prepared to support their continued insistence that they should be treated as before. But however much they say they can understand our frustrations, their actions tell a different story. To get change we have to persuade these people to change and to do this requires them to accept the need for change. The way the system of capital ownership, control and decision-making operates today there are few if any significant reasons why those at the top of large corporations will do anything more than sympathize with our concerns and keep on making the same decisions. In their world nothing has changed: they can still point to apparent talent shortages, to market pressures and to broad investor approval to support the inexorable movement upwards of the costs of employment. The reason for this continuing divergence is structural and it sits behind much of what went wrong in financial services in 2007/8.

CAPITAL MARKETS

When Queen Elizabeth II went to the London School of Economics in the aftermath of the near meltdown her words resonated with many ordinary people: 'Why did nobody notice it?'[1] She spoke for everyone. If anyone had been prepared to give her an honest answer it would have been this: 'We were warned, but we failed to listen because we were making too much money and didn't want to change'. The signs had been around for a while and there was no shortage of people trying to get leaders to accept the need for change; the challenge was to find a leader who wanted to hear what was being said.

In 2003 a conference was held at Harvard Business School entitled 'Restoring Trust in American Business'.[2] The keynote address was given by D. Quinn Mills, the Alfred J. Weatherhead, Jr Professor of Business Administration, Emeritus, at Harvard Business School. In it he asserted that the US securities industry was broken and whilst he, like so many others at the time, had confidence in the banks he was worried that unless the securities industry addressed some key issues they would run the risk of undermining the US economy.

Mills argued that capital markets required four qualities from those who participate in them: honesty, disclosure, transparency and professionalism. 'Those are missing now, and those are exactly the qualities that are needed before we'll see any significant change in the prevailing lack of trust', he said. The two specific examples of the issues that needed to be resolved that he highlighted were remuneration practices prevalent across industries in the US (and more widely in the UK and other major developed economies) and institutionalized conflicts of interest that were not being challenged and addressed.

The conflicts Mills raised five years before the global crisis have sat at the heart of the plummeting in trust of business and its leaders across the world: conflicts between chief executives and their shareholders; banks and customers' investments; and auditors and boards of directors and their shareholders. These have been well rehearsed. Yet Mills also suggested three others that he felt were as important but less talked about. The first was the attitudes and behaviour of the modern generation of venture capitalists who he argued were far too short-term compared to their predecessors and who, because they often raised their money from others, were under pressure to engineer a rapid financial improvement in performance and then return the company to the market, cashing in and getting out before any bad news could come along to reduce their returns.

The second and third areas of conflict concerned the relationship between business and wider civil society. He described the first of these as a conflict between politicians and the public. Politicians have to raise money 'from these same people who have done so well by defrauding investors', he said. In any democratic system of government the costs of getting elected have spiralled as politicians strive to out-do each other in getting their messages to the electorate. The final conflict concerned non-profit organizations 'like our own universities, museums, churches – whose leaders should be talking about this, and talking about it more than they are, who should be providing some of the ethical [discussions], but who are out there with their tin cups raising money from the very people that they would otherwise be called upon to criticize and condemn'.

These were prescient comments. The rise of the power and influence of private equity houses in North America and Europe in the middle of the first decade of the 21st century has been a powerful driver of change. Whilst much of that change has been positive, some of if was not. The positives are well promoted by the sector: R&D investment in UK companies owned through private equity grew by 14% per annum in the five years to 2006/7 as opposed to 1% per annum nationally; sales revenues grew at above average levels in the same period; and the contribution to UK taxation revenues was over £35 billion. Nearly 8% of the UK's workforce in 2008 was employed in companies owned by private equity investors.[3]

The negatives, however, have also been significant, in particular the highly leveraged positions that these organizations have imposed on their investments. After the dot-com bubble burst and interest rates were cut to significantly lower levels opponents have argued that private equity became more aggressive, particularly in the leveraged buyout market where funds furnish a small proportion of the acquisition price and borrow the rest. In recent years, private equity they claim has borrowed bigger amounts, often to provide attractive dividends. They complain that instead of spending time re-organizing a company, some acquisitions have been sold on after less than a year, sparking accusations of greed.

In May 2007 *Business Week* reported that in the United States the average debt-level in private equity deals was approaching 5.9 times cash flow with debt multiples as high as eight or nine times.[4] They cited two deals as examples: the $8.2 billion deal for media giant Tribune which involved a two-part plan to acquire outstanding shares and left the company with as much as $13 billion in debt

– ten times its cash flow; and the Alltel $27.5 billion deal where the company's debt ratio rose to about eight times earnings before interest, taxes, depreciation and amortization (known as EBITDA). These would be regarded as a very risky investment position by any high street bank being asked to finance a local company. Indeed I doubt if I showed any well trained bank manager these figures that I would get their backing. Yet somehow it seems that the size of the numbers and therefore the size of the benefits reduced the risk for banks and investors who would in the past have shunned this type of opportunity. Indeed deals like this abounded because of their scale due to the ability, for everyone involved, in putting these deals together to gain a fee. The lawyers, the investment bankers, commercial advisers and others all added their charges to the cost of the debt, and with big sums come equally big charges.

The trend was clear and the consequences, unless lending behaviour changed in banking, were clearly understood and accepted amongst those with the power to bring about change.

At the time of this report, near the apex of the credit bubble and just a few months before it burst with such traumatic consequences, an increasing number of investors were predicting a big wave of credit defaults, yet the market continued to lend and to support these highly leveraged positions. This bullish attitude, in face of a considerable body of economic theory, was based on an argument that higher leverage ratios were acceptable because low interest rates and a healthy business environment meant that many stronger companies could afford to take on high debt without incurring unmanageable risk. The same *Business Week* article drew attention to a May 2007 report from Citigroup arguing that '[a] path to higher risk and leverage is visible for the corporate sector amid the private equity buying binge. However, this remains a path to be trod.' Leaving aside the bad syntax, this report is revealing in two ways: that a major bank was happy to support a very benign view of risk, the report itself was titled 'Leverage & Growth – Get Used to Them Both', and that this was clearly the same principle they applied to their own business: Citigroup is the only major bank in the United States to be bailed out by the government twice in thirty years.[5]

There was a view prevalent at the time that even weaker companies could live with high debt. The market believed that there were few loan conditions that could trigger a default – and if they got into trouble, someone else was always there to lend them more money. *Business Week* quotes one investor as saying:

> I see a tremendous amount of liquidity in the financial system and no signs of it drying up. Even if companies hit 'speed bumps,' it will be a while before they run into problems with their lenders. I think the only thing that changes this is if there is complete re-pricing of risk across all asset classes – debt, equity, real estate, etc.[6]

This is an extraordinary report. Any economic historian reading it would have spotted all the aspects of a credit and investment bubble, indeed very similar views were expressed at the height of Tulipomania, Missouri Madness and the South Sea Bubble. The doomsday scenario, as it is in any credit bubble, is when the money runs out: whether this comes from a price crash as with tulips or a liquidity freeze as in France, the risk was understood but not priced in, nor hedged nor mitigated. It was right out there and no-one in the epicentre of the bubble thought it could ever hit them unless it were an act of God or Al Quaeda.

As in the greatest of Greek tragedies or in the best of Shakespeare, after hubris comes nemesis. Those making money from these financial gymnastics didn't notice that they were soon to be the authors of their own cataclysmic event through their selling and re-selling of high risk financial products that it turned out none of them really understood.

POLITICS AND CIVIL SOCIETY

Regarding politicians Mills hit the nail on the head here as well. The thirst of politicians for funds through which to win office or retain it can no longer be slaked by the funding raised through the membership of their political parties. Whilst President Obama made a virtue out of not reaching out to big business and the captains of industry during his 2008 campaign for the White House he still managed to spend more than any other contender in history: a staggering $650 million.

Even for the vast majority of politicians who don't possess the President's charisma the tap is still there to be turned. In Africa, in Europe or in Asia, big business and its agenda can gain a hearing through the funding of individuals and political parties. Whether this is through the funding of election campaigns or the funding of regional/local community projects in countries where elections are not contested but community bases are critical for continued access to the fruits of power business finds a way of making itself heard by those in power.

Regardless of the system, political influence could always and can still be bought. As the funding requirements for political success get greater and greater, so the opportunity for businesses, and even more specifically business leaders, to acquire influence and preferment, either in policy or personally, continues to exist. The system of highly developed political parties that exists in the vast majority of developed countries provides the perfect vehicle for that influence to be brought to bear. Party preferment is the way to political power for individuals and the way most individuals find money to support their election ambitions. Funding the party brings connection and connection brings the opportunity to influence.

In the UK over the past two centuries the only thing that has really altered in the business of politics is that patronage has passed from the monarch to the head of government and the use of executive power at the expense of parliament created a small and powerful elite whose connections to those with money run deep. In 1997 Tony Blair raised over £1 million from business,[7] and considerably more from wealthy individual donors who had made their money in business. To attract such donors, many of whom had previously supported the Conservative party, the Labour party established an organization linked to business where membership benefits included access to shadow ministers and their advisers and after the election this translated into access to government ministers and their advisers. Labour's £1 million donation from Bernie Ecclestone, the Formula One entrepreneur and the subsequent proposal by the Labour government to reprieve that business from a ban on income from tobacco sponsorship was an early example of the party's seemingly inexhaustible attraction to celebrity businessmen which subsequently brought reputational damage.[8]

In the list of regular backers were not just ordinary businesses, but those most associated with the corporate excesses of the last twenty years. For example, in 1997 and 1998 it is claimed that Enron donated around £30,000.[9] Many have argued that Labour's approach to media ownership and their determination to clip the wings of the BBC was due to Rupert Murdoch's support for the party in all of his major titles in 1997 and again in 2001 and 2005. Murdoch and his media business in the UK had taken a very aggressive position on the state broadcaster as they moved into television with the acquisition of a significant stake in the satellite TV broadcast network, BSkyB. The shift Murdoch has made in his titles to supporting the Conservative party in 2010 is already raising questions about the bill that will be paid now they are the majority party in the coalition government.

Mills' final targets were people like me: deans of business schools, presidents and vice chancellors of universities, head teachers of major schools. We were accused of being too busy attracting corporate funding and corporate business to speak without fear or favour and challenge what some of us at least knew to be happening. In Europe I believe there are schools with a tradition of a very strong ethical and 'values-led' perspective. I also believe that these are the exception to the rule in a sector which, like many others, saw the corporate gravy train as a source of income which could keep it away from the need for a much more searching examination of its faults and flaws. Like some others in the sector my colleagues and I have held a very critical position on the behaviour that we believe has damaged the reputation of business in general from the early 2000s. However, for the big US business schools and those who have adopted their model in Europe, this is a fair challenge. They provided the talent that created the intellectual property that was sold on through the investment chain only to become 'toxic debt'. They took the money from the men and women who made a fortune from the deals and reinvested it in courses and curricula that reinforced what is now known to be a vicious circle. As educators they became the antithesis of all that Aristotle argued for in the preparation required for a virtuous leader. There is much still to argue about in business education in general and business schools in particular. However, it is important for the sector that it recognizes some of the practices that contributed to the feeding frenzy of the 1990s and 2000s. In particular the role played by rankings and their reliance on salary increases as a measure of return on investment. Also, the over-dominance of finance-based courses and the under representation of micro-economics and business history and the practice, still unchecked, of taking students with less and less work experience and selling them into big jobs with all the theory but none of the required understanding. The decision of Harvard Business School to admit candidates to its MBA programme[10] with no work experience at all is a significant example of the willingness of the sector to validate the 'get rich quick' aspirations of future business leaders that the L'Oreal generation had established as the norm.

It is worth pausing at this point to reflect on two other Harvard contributions to business education. The first, for which they are famous, is the 'case study' approach to education which is now a relatively standard method in many business schools worldwide. This model of education takes a business problem from the past, encourages the class to study and review it and to come up with solutions. Having prepared the case there follows a gladiatorial contest of intellects in front of a Professor as rival solutions are debated and challenged. At the end they discover who was right when the Professor pronounces the solution. This system of education works in two circumstances. Either where there is little or no experience in the room of this problem such that a reality has to be constructed within which to explore the application of theory (with all the attendant caveats of this is theoretical and clearly practice will be different). Or where, regardless of experience, the circumstances in the world are such that the time gap between the case being written and the student putting this learning into practice is irrelevant. The pace of change in business today means that

very little of practical value outside of classic issues such as motivation or the basics of accounting and importance of cash can be
gained from studying a case that is older than probably a year or
so, maybe two to three at the outside. Despite this, top schools
persist in using it to turn out young people who think they know
the answers and succeed in getting them placed in big jobs where
their over-confidence can have a major impact. This in turn validates the systemic assumption that bright graduates from top
business schools are the only really talented people worth recruiting and reinforces their 'rarity value' in the market. To change the
mindset of their graduate output from the certainty that created
the financial crisis to an acceptance of fallibility and a curiosity to
find out and value the views of others will require a wholesale
rejection of the case method.

The second contribution is a consequence of the crisis itself: the
proposed 'ethical oath'. This has been championed by some at
Harvard as the answer to the problem: a business equivalent of the
Hippocratic Oath taken by all medical students as they graduate
into practising doctors. It came from students themselves, which
should tell us something about the problems of being very bright
but not having any real experience within which to set your potential answers to real life problems and has found champions in such
as Niall Ferguson amongst many others.[11] It fails the test for so
many reasons. Management is not a profession; there are no professional bodies with sanctions that can act on a public complaint of
'violation' of the oath. Standards for acceptability of behaviour in
business differ hugely across cultures. Interpretation of motivation
is unbelievably difficult, as anyone who deals with grievances and
disputes at work will testify, and proving deliberate intent to act

unethically in the majority of cases that might be heard I suspect would be downright impossible. This proposal is fanciful and diverts attention away from the real issues in business education. It says a great deal about the value placed on their education by these students that they feel that they have to promise to apply it ethically: in my view a good education delivers an ethical perspective without having recourse to something akin to the motto of the Scout Movement.

The one thing I would agree on with the proponents of the oath, however, is that at the heart of the problem is the behaviour of those in the financial services sector in particular. It is important to understand how this was shaped by the structural changes that occurred over the last thirty years or so. This is not a book on the financial crisis but it is worth looking at three aspects. First, the implications for management practice of the amalgamation of the more entrepreneurial trading activities with high street retail banking and financial services. Secondly, the changes to the competitive environment and the impact this had on organizations far less used to the management of significant levels of risk. Thirdly, the transformation in the availability of credit to fund 'lifestyles' that until the 1980s were beyond the reach of the ordinary working man and woman. Finally, the introduction of the concept of a 'limited liability partnership'.

DEREGULATION AND DEBT

In the 1980s The City and other global financial centres witnessed a transformation in financial services. This saw the tearing down of the old boundaries that separated at one end the unlimited liability partnerships who dominated share broking, the insurance market and investment banking, from at the other end the limited liability companies who delivered retail banking and the mutual sector who provided mortgage services. In the UK the deregulation was radical and this allowed for significant degrees of conglomeration creating giant organizations with vastly different internal cultures and attitudes to such things as lending and investment risk. Whilst in terms of people employed and numbers of customers the retail banking, mortgage and domestic insurance businesses of these organizations were significant, in terms of contribution to profitability it was the high risk end of the operation that dominated.[12] Critical to retaining this profitability was the retention of the highly entrepreneurial employees that had been acquired with the buying up of previously unlimited liability partnerships. These people had swapped the uncertainty of employment in a partnership that, if it failed to judge and manage risk appropriately or if it failed to retain sufficient cash to cover a bad year, could go bust with no compensation and with considerable personal liability for the partners, for one where they could still operate in the much more risky investment markets but with the protection of the limited liability ownership structure of a retail bank or former mutual. What had happened, without any real owner consultation or understanding, was therefore the continuation of the generous rewards associated with the successful taking of significant risks with considerable personal liability as a brake on excessive behaviour in either risk taking or in the amount of money taken out of the business for personal reward. This is the antithesis of limited liability cultures with a wide shareowner base where the bulk of the rewards went to the owners who took the financial risk whilst the managers were far better protected in terms of personal liability and the provision of long-term benefits such as a good pension. As one part of the bank started earning considerably more than the other so this drove a significant upgrading of top executive salaries, regardless of activity managed and the creation of much more entrepreneurial reward structures which in turn drove increasingly risky business practices. The failure to spot, address or resolve this issue is at the heart of much of the public sense of outrage about bankers' bonuses. This is well illustrated by the story of Northern Rock.

At the heart of the UK's Northern Rock debacle – the first run on a UK bank for 140 years – lies an uncomfortable truth: remuneration strategies that are constructed to deliver significant monetary rewards with no link to value creation and strategic goals almost always deliver the wrong results for everyone else. It is also totemic of the impact of a shift in values that was accelerating a head-long rush into conspicuous consumption.

The Rock Building Society and the Northern Counties Permanent Building Society were early examples of mutual saving and loans societies. Their very names chosen to reflect to potential customers the prudence, steadfastness and reliability they expected from a vehicle that was to take hard earned savings – often taken from meagre pay-packets at great sacrifice – and to turn these into affordable loans with which could be purchased property. They were established in the 19th century in the wake of major pressure for political reform to provide working people with access to property and the power and control over their own lives that came with it.

The building society movement sprung from the friendly societies of the late 18th century when working men began to pool their funds in organizations from which they could borrow to build houses. Property was not the only sector of the economy to benefit from mutuality. Mutuality was a successful and popular business model in the 19th and 20th century: well-known organizations such as the Co-operative Society started out as mutual societies and the Co-op and a few remaining building societies retain their mutuality as a differentiator today: their values reflecting the virtues that they believe a social enterprise can bring.

What was interesting about the mutual movement in any sector was that it saw a way in which to apply the market as a mechanism through which their members would improve their financial and social position: at the time many were formed, the ownership of property brought with it political as well as financial clout under a restricted franchise which reserved voting in parliamentary and municipal elections to the property-owning classes. What the founders of the mutual movement wanted to do was to get the market to work for ordinary people as well as for the capital-owning class. They used the returns they got for their enterprise as savings and ultimately deposits for investment in bricks and mortar.

The demutualizing of the UK's building societies during the last two decades of the 20th century is one of the great examples of the shift in values from enterprise as the generator of wealth for all to self-interest as the generator of wealth: it signals the coming of age of the L'Oreal generation. The demise of building societies and the cranking up of retail and commercial banks into large finance houses with a far greater tolerance of risk over this period contains within it the genesis of the catastrophe of 2008. These changes in the UK stemmed from the changes that had happened in post-war British society that re-shaped attitudes to financial affairs.

Nearly thirty years ago the Thatcher government in Britain set about a policy of significant economic liberalization. Whilst much of this reform has set the foundation for the UK's relative economic success until recent years, their liberalization of the financial sector has been more controversial. Not least because some of the outcomes are now making economists and politicians alike very uncomfortable.

A dramatic example was the rise in the level of personal debt. Let me illustrate this with a few statistics:[13]

- Total UK personal debt at the end of December 2009 stood at **£1,460 billion.**
- This had increased 0.7% in the last 12 months, despite all the predictions of debt repayment.
- Personal debt as a proportion of average earnings as at December 2009 stood at 129%.
- Average household debt in the UK was £9,000 (excluding mortgages).
- This figure increases to £18,722 if the average is based on the number of households who actually have some form of unsecured loan.
- Average household debt in the UK was £57,937 (including mortgages).

- If you added personal debt to the December 2009 pre budget report figure for public sector net debt (PSND) expected in 2014–15 (excluding financial interventions) then this figure rose to £116,390 per household.
- Average owed by every UK adult was £30,252 (including mortgages).
- One person in the UK was declared bankrupt or insolvent every 3.5 minutes.

The increasing appetite for debt in the 1990s and the business opportunities this presented banks and other financial institutions were very tempting. This set the wheels in motion for Northern Rock's transformation into a bank. By borrowing more than they could as a building society they could lend more and through lending more they could make money, especially in a rising market. Their rise and fall can be put at the door of one of their biggest selling products: the 'Together' loan. This allowed someone to borrow as much as 125% of a property's value, plus up to six times annual income. This seemed like a great idea – but only if the value of residential houses in the UK property market and the incomes of borrowers were going to rise. Not only did they have to rise but they had to do so fast enough such that the multiple borrowed against house value and income reduced reasonably rapidly and payments became affordable. Historically any prudent assessment of the riskiness of these two assumptions holding good for the first few years of such a loan should have sounded all the alarm bells for a competent management and board of directors and what happened showed just how risky this assumption was.[14]

The UK's Land Registry reports show that over the period 2007–2010, average house prices moved from £175,000 in 2007 to £155,000 in 2009 to £165,000 in 2010. The impact on lower earners who had been encouraged to take out large loans to fund their purchases in the expectation of ever increasing asset values was significant. The impact on the banks who lent this money was disastrous.

The crash came early to Northern Rock because its funding of this rapid growth in mortgage lending was based on a business model that left it more exposed than the rest to the impact of equally poor management practice in the US mortgage market. The consequences for its borrowers who couldn't cope with the impact of the recession that followed were dire.[15] The consequences for those who have clung on and whose property value has fallen and whose wages have not increased facing the prospect of rising interest rates could be even more so.

What underpinned this reckless drive for growth was not only the personal ambition of those leading the company but also the structural changes that took the culture of the trading room into the world of the retail bank. The remuneration plan approved by the directors for the CEO and senior executives was very simple: it rewarded ever increasing levels of mortgage lending and encouraged ever increasing multiples and ever increasing risk. Whilst much of the coverage has focused on the role of the CEO the role of the non-executive directors too has to come into question. Whilst some may have had banking backgrounds, they brought very different perspectives, including those from the UK's hedge fund industry, which were a long way away from the background and values of the founders of the original mutual. Yet it was these original values which I believe the vast majority of investors and borrowers had assumed were still in place because of the heritage of reliability bestowed by their reputation.

Their former mutuality implied a level of prudence in management practice which was very far from the truth. As the financial system unwound around the world so more and more of these practices, in North America, in Europe and beyond were exposed.

In the latter half of 2008 a parade of banking executives appeared before the US Senate Banking Committee and were reduced to monosyllabic replies as details of their earnings were laid bare alongside their inability to explain or apologize for their actions. Bankers across Europe have lost their jobs and forfeited their bonus plans as governments bailed out their balance sheets and rescued global liquidity. Probably the most astounding revelation relating to that year was the admission of the directors of the US insurance giant AIG during a House of Representatives' hearing that one of their last actions as a board of a failing organization was to hold a remuneration committee to restructure the rules surrounding their remuneration so that they could secure their bonus payments and fund them as a result of the government injection of cash that kept their company afloat. The political storm that followed revealed a trail of venality that stunned even the most hardened of Wall Street observers. The letter from the New York Attorney General to the House Committee on Financial Services lays out a $160 million transfer of funds from the company to senior executives of whom seventy-three each took home $1 million or more.[16]

STEWARDSHIP, PARTNERSHIP AND LIABILITY

So as a result of the structural integration of all aspects of financial services into a single organization we conflated the very important distinction between being an entrepreneur and leading an enterprise on behalf of other people. This conflation has been contagious and as reward practice in financial services shifted significantly so did that of other sectors who felt that if they didn't keep up they would lose their 'top talent' or fail to attract top talent in the market place. Today's leaders of enterprise are rewarded far more like the entrepreneurs than corporate stewards.

Entrepreneurs are, however, a specialized and individualistic breed. They have a tolerance for risk far greater than the majority, they understand needs and markets and are instinctive traders. In my introduction to his classic work on entrepreneurship I make the point that Peter Drucker[17] captures the essence of entrepreneurship as not being so much a capitalist proposition, as a state of mind. Entrepreneurs can be found in all parts of society not just in that part defined as wealth-creating; what defines them is their attitude to change. In Drucker's words, 'the entrepreneur always searches for change, responds to it and exploits it as an opportunity'. It is innovation that endows resources with a new capacity to create wealth, be that personal or social. For economic entrepreneurs, there is a further differentiation in that the risk they take is tied up not just with reputation but also with the potential for personal financial loss. The point of being an economic entrepreneur is that you are prepared to risk your own capital, your own future and quite often your own family in pursuit of success. They have 'skin in the game' and whilst they take risks they are rarely reckless. After all it is their own money, and just as importantly their own reputation, that is at stake when they act. There is no one to give them a handsome severance payment and a pension pot worth millions of pounds when they fail.

The majority of us, however, are not entrepreneurs. We sell our skills to others rather than exploit them for our own benefit. We risk capital that belongs to others and our actions are far more likely to damage the reputation of the brand or public service or charitable organization than our own. The most successful of us become corporate executives and there is a very real difference here between successful entrepreneurs and corporate executives. It is the difference between ownership and stewardship. It is a very different thing to risk your own capital, your own reputation and to work hard for the rewards of success. If you are the owner then rightly you have the choice of whether to harvest the returns from your efforts or to re-invest them. That right has never been granted to a steward.

This notion of a steward is one tied up with our cultural and social development in Europe. It is an altruistic role, looking after and protecting the assets of others. Whilst there are benefits through doing this to the steward, the greatest benefit of good stewarding goes to others – the owner of the land and their tenants. European literature is full of references to good and bad stewardship from Homer through Shakespeare to Chekov and Thomas Mann. This shared cultural inheritance has helped to define a shared perspective of the responsibility to others that ownership of a key asset and its direction demands.

In the European model of management, corporate managers are not owners: they are stewards. It is not their wealth, their property or their futures they put at risk. Since the end of the Second World

War this view has lost currency in North American business and business education. Here the individual is more prominent and this positive value has been stretched and twisted to support the fallacious proposition that managers themselves bring their 'talent' to the assets employed and that this talent is worth as much (if not more) to any enterprise as the capital invested in it. The spread of individualism as a shared value in business leaders can be mapped alongside the movement of North American corporations across the globe. As they bring their employment and reward practices and put them into new geographies so these geographies develop similar attitudes and behaviours and the data shows us that they are now prevalent at the top of many European businesses, particularly in the global arena of financial services.

In this conglomeration in the financial services sector I have argued that investors are as much to blame for the outcome as those they left in charge of their capital. The real owner, the individual whose money is often placed in the pension fund, the insurance policy, the investment fund and then invested on their behalf by an 'expert' is in my view far less culpable. The separation of the interests of the owners of the capital employed from the management of the corporation is a result of the radical change in the dynamics of the ownership structures in capital markets. Even in the 1970s it was still the case that shareholders were predominantly wealthy individuals. In the United States institutional holdings as opposed to individual holdings represented 19% of stock. In 2005 it was reported that the largest one hundred money managers in the US control 52% of all US equity. In the UK whilst private individuals owned 54% of UK stocks in 1963 twenty years later this had reduced to less than 15%.[18]

This consolidation was accelerated by the deregulation of capital markets in the 1980s on both sides of the Atlantic which, as I have shown, spawned mega-banks with global reach and operations at every stage of the capital value chain. These organizations controlled the market from both sides of capital transactions and removed the age-old market self-regulating mechanism of separate buyers and sellers of stocks and shares. Reduced capital holding requirements in banks threw off far greater liquidity than before and this amongst other things created more capital for higher risk activities. One consequence of this was the explosion in the number and impact of hedge funds (an invention from the late 1950s in the United States to avoid the regulatory constraints placed on mutual funds) from a very specialist fringe activity into a global phenomenon running in a shadow financial system which operated in an opaque environment with unclear regulation and little trust. Indeed both these structural changes led to the creation of a system that failed to meet any of Professor Mills' requirements for a healthy and effective capital market.

The biggest beneficiary of this consolidation however was the 'fund manager'. These individuals control the bulk of the holdings for most listed companies. They are the people who cast their votes in favour or against resolutions at an annual general meeting and they do so on their own judgement, without any obligation to consult with or be informed by the opinions of those whose capital they are managing and from whom they take a fixed percentage for administration. And what is more, they do so regardless of their success. There is no performance related pay in fund management, in the most part the rewards come from the size of the assets under control so the incentive is to bring in new funds every year over and above losses from the fund either through funds being withdrawn or from a loss in value as a result of market movement or poor investment choices. Given in reality that many of these funds are so-called tracker funds with a very large spread of holdings many fund managers are really paid a great deal for nothing more than competent administration.

The fund managers, given they are employed by organizations that have the same reward structures and principles as those being presented to them, are far less likely to baulk at the overall size of the take from the owner – after all they are not owners themselves. They are much more exercised about paying these rewards where fund returns are negatively impacted such that their own remuneration (driven by fund value under management) is negatively impacted. This is hardly a recipe for a healthy, long-term engagement with a business where there is a wish for the business to succeed as a whole rather than for a singular and narrow focus on shareholder value.

So what the media call 'investors' are not really investors at all: they are advisers with none of their own skin in the game. Often working to completely contradictory purposes from those who entrust them with their capital, their decisions will be driven by their needs for liquidity, for profits and to achieve targets in their own highly leveraged incentive plans. Whilst there are some remaining long-term investment funds, more and more of the shares in publicly quoted companies in developed economies are owned by those with high risk profiles whose business models drive costs that demand increasingly higher returns from investments to ameliorate the much higher risk profiles and a track record that looks far less successful than their popular reputation.[19]

Alongside these aspects of structural change has sat the introduction of the concept of a limited liability partnership. This ema-
nated from the US where it was introduced in Texas in the
aftermath of another banking collapse, in order to protect 'innocent
partners' in law and accounting firms from personal bankruptcy
following claims to recoup losses linked to their professional advice.
By the late 1990s most states had legislation in place permitting
this form of incorporation. It was introduced into the UK through
the Limited Liability Partnership Acts 2000 and 2002 and in most
EU and other major economies during the early part of the 21st
century.[20] This radically altered the basis on which advisory firms
such as lawyers, auditors and accountants operated and could be
held liable for their actions. In the UK there developed a principle
in law where an individual partner is liable for no more than the
value of their initial investment in the partnership in the settlement
of any claim against it.[21] In the US the model adopted by the
majority of states is subtly but importantly different in that the
partnership is liable but not any one member of it. In other words
the partnership is now treated as having no more liability than that
of a company. This in one stroke changed the contract between the
partners within the firm and between the firm and its clients.
When all partners held unlimited liability they policed their peers
so as to ensure that the best possible advice was offered and prudent
actions were taken on behalf of clients. They protected themselves
against risk of a liability either by holding value within the partnership rather than distributing all of it to partners or through individual partners building up their own reserves to cover personal
risk. They understood the risk they were taking and behaved
accordingly. They were collective entrepreneurs with all the risks

and the personal benefits that came with it. With the introduction of the LLP individual liability has either virtually or completely disappeared. This is an interesting concept: one where firms can continue to exist without the public scrutiny and oversight demanded of limited liability public companies. They can act as a partnership and share the profits at the end of the financial year with far less provision for liability than previously would have been the case. Indeed to quote one of the leading experts in the UK:

> It's a more flexible vehicle than a limited company. For example, its tax treatment is more akin to a partnership and that in many ways is more attractive than for a limited company/employee type arrangement.
>
> And you can agree pretty much what you want to do in a LLP without reference to others, like shareholders.[22]

What he is really saying is that their partners can generate the returns associated with high levels of risk without any significant liability falling on them as individuals should those risks impact adversely on the firm or its clients. Whilst the rise of the global firm has been followed by the rise of the global advisor, the vehicle that allows advisors this very privileged position is an anomaly. I believe that it is stoking risk in the system as there are few checks or balances that can regulate their interventions.

This chapter has looked at the structural and governance issues that contributed to the position we now find ourselves in with regard to the leadership of the modern corporation. It has also examined how these have reinforced the perception of self-importance and enabled self-aggrandisement mainly at the expense of the real owners of the capital employed in the business.

What is critical, I believe, is to return to the very clear understanding that corporate managers are not owners: they are stewards of their owners' capital. It is not their wealth, their property or their futures they put at risk. Their real owners are often pensioners or future pensioners with few assets. Most of their employees earn around the average wage or lower. Many of the communities in which they have factories, offices and depots have few, if any, other significant sources of paid employment. The actions of corporate managers and their advisors and the decisions of those who channel owner funds into corporations have to accept new roles and new rules if they are to deliver long-term wealth creation that sustains rather than corrodes public confidence in the market.

In the last two decades, the UK and US governments have made some efforts to address rising public concerns over the behaviour of corporate management. Especially so following the spectacular collapses of Marconi, Enron, Tyco and Worldcom and the outcry amongst investors over the rising value of CEO and other executive remuneration packages. The 2002 Sarbanes-Oxley Act in the US and the UK's 2002 Directors' Remuneration Report Regulations and 2006 Companies Act tightened risk management and reporting requirements. In the UK the regulations required executive remuneration reports to be voted upon separately and introduced the concept of a board taking a broader view of transactions and responsibilities (enlightened shareholder responsibility) than just the purely financial. However, with increasing amounts of business activities being owned by private rather than public companies and with investors looking for increasingly speculative returns these well-intentioned legislative interventions seemed to have little impact. After all, despite them we suffered the biggest ever collapse in a global business sector and have continued to watch the remuneration packages of business leaders spiral ever-upwards.

Despite the ambitions of political leaders to create a share-owning democracy, today in the vast majority of developed economies we have transformed the ownership of capital from one share-owning autocracy to another. The difference between the old autocrats and the new is, however, striking. The new autocrats are getting rich through the administration of the capital of others rather than through risking their own. The system has to reassert the primacy of the owner and has to find ways for the real owners to make the impact felt.

Chapter Four
The Public Gets What
the Public Wants
Values, Confidence, Trust and Reputation
in Leadership

The impact of the L'Oreal generation as leaders has been portrayed by some as a consequence of unbridled capitalism and of our meek and misguided acceptance that the market is the only realistic option for generating wealth in society.[1] Had we operated another economic or social system, they argue, we would not have had the banking excesses and the eventual financial consequences for our nations and for our own pockets. However, before we cast ourselves in the role of helpless victim and criticize the failure in leadership we need to remember that in many places in this world we the consumer, the citizen, the voter give these other people power to exercise on our behalf. Whether it is our lack of interest in and engagement with politics; our disinterested investments in insurance policies, share plans and savings schemes; our purchasing of newspapers and TV channels regardless of the use their owners make of our money or our commitment to brands despite their employment practices and their exploitation of suppliers we act every day to give support and succour to those whom we then criticize.

The shift in values mapped out in Chapter Two has under-pinned the development of a society whose guiding purpose is consumption. Whilst there is some evidence that this view is being rejected, especially by younger generations, it is this view that still predominates with the majority of those in leadership positions today. In this society there is no sense of restraint, no sense that there are finite limitations in for example, energy resources from fossil fuels or to the supply of fresh water. The majority of consumers don't stop to worry about the sourcing of the raw materials or the processes through which this product was created. This society does not see the need to balance population with resources, with space and with land that can sustain cultivation or be used for animals. It throws objects away, not just because they are broken but because there are now better products available to do the same job or simply because they are no longer fashionable. This is in one sense the apex of the consumer society: we no longer work to live, we work to sustain a 'lifestyle' which is defined by what we consume. Where this behaviour and attitude to material possessions was the preserve of the very wealthy in developed societies in the 19th century and the first half of the 20th (and arguably much more recently than this in parts of the European Union) it is now a reality for the majority of citizens of the developed world.[2]

It is however not a problem of one social or political system. In China the emergence of a middle class has created an imperative for sustained economic growth that is now consuming even more of the world's finite resources than ever before. Even in Cuba[3] the need for foreign currency has created a consumer culture in Havana and other tourist destinations that is heavily influenced by the

United States. Aspiration is a powerful part of the human condition and as aspirations move from social and political goals to economic ones so it seems the motivators and incentives converge regardless of the political and economic regime. Increasingly we see a sense of individualism gaining the upper hand over the inevitably more constraining collective point of view. Whilst the dominant value set in any society is one of economic self-improvement with no concern for the relative position of others, then the behaviour we have rightly criticized of investment bankers in the US and the UK will be equally present in the emerging middle classes in India, China, Russia and Brazil. Whilst new and more socially and environmentally aware value sets are emerging they are, as yet, still a minority perspective. Political leaders are beginning to think about the longer-term impact of what is happening as a result of this headlong rush into mass consumption and how the world will have to change it habits in energy consumption, scarce resource utilization, population control and food production. Meanwhile, those in the wealth creating sector are well placed to lead through changes they could make now to reduce their impact on the planet and to change human behaviour, whilst still creating wealth. Whether we act as owners, customers and consumers or as concerned citizens what we have to get business to embrace is the importance of value and values in the creation of a sustainable wealth creating sector. A wealth-creating sector which doesn't just focus on rewards at the top, but thinks about impact right through the value chain.

An important element of business reform, therefore, is to encourage business to think and act in a longer-term way. This means accepting the importance of measures of success in addition to those that are purely 12-month (or even shorter in the quarterly reporting requirements in the US) and financial. This is a major change programme and has to happen at the same time as the changes in the manifesto that forms the second part of the book. To do this requires an understanding of four related concepts and how they play a role in business success: reputation; trust; confidence and values.

REPUTATION

Ultimately, an organization is at its most effective when it has a positive reputation with the majority of its stakeholders. Its stakeholders range from those most immediately associated with its success: owners, employees, suppliers and customers, to those impacted by its operations and its products or services. These would include government, local communities, the media and NGOs. The reputation of any organization is the most difficult intangible to measure and the most challenging to manage. However, without it, the organization eventually loses the right to operate. Firms go out of business, governments lose elections and chief executives are sacked because their reputation fails.

The work done by the John Madejski Centre for Reputation[4] in exploring the role of reputation in building long-term corporate success has made a significant contribution to the development of a model of how leaders can think through to the longer term. Significantly, what they have been able to demonstrate is how what leaders do today impacts on the reputation of the organization they lead and its performance over the medium to long term. Called the 'SPIRIT' model, (Figure 4.1) it provides a framework through which leaders can understand the impact of their actions on their reputation in the eyes of each of their major stakeholders.

The model suggests that the future behaviour of stakeholders towards a business is built on how they currently feel about the business (i.e. their attitudes). This, in turn, is derived from the way the business has affected them directly in the past, or through the influence of contextual factors such as reporting in the media, hearing or reading the opinions of influential people or the actions or comments of competitors.

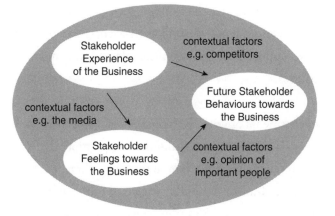

Figure 4.1 'The SPIRIT Model'

An organization can build an understanding of its reputation in the eyes of its stakeholders and in identifying the drivers of that reputation can work to build support and long-term commitment. To do this requires an in-depth exploration of three areas:

- **Stakeholder experience of the business** defined as stakeholder experience and perception of a business in terms of important relationship issues. These include the various kinds of benefits (material and nonmaterial) offered to stakeholders and how stakeholders judge the past behaviour of the business.

- **Stakeholder attitudes (trust and emotions towards the business)** are at the core of good relationships. The measure of these attitudes includes the perceived reliability and dependability of a business and also indicates whether stakeholders have positive or negative feelings towards the business.

- **Stakeholder support of the business** is a key indicator of the future success of a business. Measures provide an indication of whether stakeholders will extend the scope of exchanges (e.g. buy different things), remain loyal, seek collaborative and innovative opportunities, recommend, defend and not harm the business.

These elements can then be linked to factors such as the impact of the media, pressure groups and the competition.

This proposition is important in two ways. First, it validates the importance to leaders of building trust and confidence in all stakeholders as a route to sustained long-term success. Secondly, it provides us with confirmation that value and values are complementary rather than conflicting propositions. Whilst reputation comes from a series of factors far wider than purely financial performance, research shows us that a positive reputation is the foundation stone for the delivery of the maximum economic value for the owners of a corporation. What is critical about this concept of 'reputation' is that it can only be judged in terms of whether the perceptions of stakeholders make them feel good about the corporation and importantly for performance, that they choose to support it as a customer or consumer or investor and as an advocate for others to do likewise.

This requires business to measure far more than their annual financial performance and to think far more innovatively about linking leadership rewards with reputational outcomes over the longer term. It implies a measurement and public reporting of the supportive or unsupportive behaviour of stakeholders towards the business. A recent paper from the Centre[5] suggested that these areas should be:

- customer satisfaction and loyalty;
- employee commitment and engagement;
- non-exploitative supplier relations;
- community trust in the business;
- environmental responsibility.

The belief is that this level of reporting should be a legal requirement. This would result in valuable data for owners and potential new investors as well as regulators and legislators which would form a far stronger indicator of future performance than relying solely on the financials. Good businesses already collect this data, or the vast majority of it; they just fail to share it with their owners. Requiring consistent reporting of such data is another powerful way of binding the stewards of the enterprise more closely to the interests of the owner.

In my view this is what the leaders of some of the world's banks and other businesses failed to understand. Whilst in business, as opposed to the world of public policy, there is no validity in the proposition a business should adopt a particular moral or ethical perspective because it is right. There is validity in adopting such a perspective because it is a driver of long-term value maximization.

This is not just an academic concept, albeit a well established one. It is already being mirrored in changes to share ownership, corporate governance and the role of the institutional investor. In the book *The New Capitalists* the authors argued that we were seeing the emergence of a 'new' capitalism. The thesis goes as follows:[6]

Individual shareowners – the new capitalists – are awakening to citizen investor power around the world, spurring Institutional investors to adopt responsible portfolio and activist strategies which prompt boards of directors to embrace sweeping reform and making them accountable to shareowners, creating an agenda for Corporations and corporate executives, who are turning to a new 'capitalist-manifesto' path to corporate success, which in turn, hands the new capitalists unprecedented clout.

At the time of its first publication I appeared on a BBC World Service discussion with one of the authors. I argued that whilst I sympathized with the model, I didn't see anything like the positive drivers for change. Nor was I confident that change would arrive unless there was a significant event where real change in share ownership and institutional investor attitudes enabled the model to gain real acceptance amongst the leaders of the corporate world. I suggested that the behaviour in the financial sector was risking just such an event. However, like everyone else I had no idea of just how bad the value system was in so much of the financial services sector.

The crash of 2008 has made the model not just a possibility, but a probable outcome if governments, who now own a significant shareholding in the world's financial system, act as responsible shareowners and stakeholders and not as the drivers of public policy. Some of the old world's constraints on a wealth-creating system acting on behalf of a greater good and not just short-term gain have gone or are going – submissive owners, marginalized or compromised regulators. However, we still exist in a world which needs to change the context for the creation of wealth, for example in blinkered accounting standards, an acceptance of the need to act sustainably and remuneration practices at the top.

Reputation then is the foundation of whether or not we choose to do business with one or other organization. It is closely related to two further important concepts: trust and confidence. The measurement of these amongst stakeholders is a key driver of reputational standing. They are, however, important in their own right and form an important element of understanding not just organizational but also personal performance.

TRUST AND CONFIDENCE

Rather like the chicken and the egg it is not clear either intuitively or from academic research which question comes first: do I trust an organization (or indeed a person) because I have confidence in it; or do I feel confident in it because I trust it (or them) to deliver. Research suggests, however, that regardless of where you start in the relationship, these are two different concepts and they can be influenced directly for good or for bad. Earlier in the book the data on trust in professions and organizations showed how little leaders in business are trusted. Work done by Professor Stephen Lee on trust and confidence in the third sector over some years has built on the significant distinction between trust and confidence and their impact on stakeholder attitudes to charitable organizations.[7] In it he and his colleagues have argued that whilst related, they drive different aspects of the reputation of an organization.

Confidence is about expectation based on experience. It links through to expertise either through prior experience of an organization or individual or through their being accredited by some form of external awarding body assessing the product or service against an independent standard.

Trust is about uncertainty, it is an expectation based on a relationship underpinned by shared values where there is no or little empirical evidence to justify belief. Yet the belief in the trusted person or organization to respond to new circumstances is such that the person trusting them does not expect to be unpleasantly surprised or upset by any response.

Both play a role in leadership. However, in the new world, increasingly, it is trust that will define leadership effectiveness supported by confidence not so much in knowledge but in the processes of how new knowledge and understandings will be created to address whatever the competitive environment throws up. Confidence in stakeholders can be built through consistent performance and a track record of competence. It can be helped in my view by a public policy agenda which sets a more transparent environment within which leaders can work. Without a response from those in government to help build a wealth-creating sector that acts sustainably and responsibly for the long-term good of all stakeholders rebuilding public confidence in the market will be far more difficult. This requires efficient and effective regulatory systems which reassure the consumer, customer, investor and supplier that in doing business with an organization there is a high degree of certainty that what they expect will be what they get. One of the issues Lee raises is a warning to business leaders not to confuse the processes of promoting confidence and trust, or to mix them up in a manner in which they try to promote or manage them. This is likely only to make things worse rather than improve them:

> Overly grandiose attempts to develop higher levels of trust, which actually focus on the elements that comprise confidence, will have little impact on the latter but further diminish the former[8]

Leaders therefore have to understand what drives trust and confidence in their own environments and how best to build them both. In so doing it is worth appreciating one significant difference between the two: trust is a relational concept. It is the instilling of faith in another human being, that when all else fails, they will continue to act positively for you or towards you. For this reason it is very difficult to have trust in an organization. You can have confidence in the National Health Service in its treatment effectiveness for a specific disease or operation through looking at recovery rates, for example. The relationship you build with a specialist can result in significant levels of trust or distrust which is far more likely to drive your behaviour in agreeing to a treatment route than any set of statistics. In leadership, therefore, personal trust in you, especially in change, is a far bigger driver of whether people will follow you and stay with you than whether or not they are completely sold on the logic of the strategy as there is little if anything in the past that can give them confidence in the future. One of the ironies of the 2008/9 financial turmoil was not that bankers and others lost our trust: banking, insurance and pension scandals had seen off any last vestiges of trust amongst stakeholders long before then. Whatever we thought of them we had confidence that they knew what they were doing: the crisis destroyed confidence and this is what has made it so difficult for governments and bankers alike trying to restore the financial system. This isn't just about restoring the value of financial services to the economies of the US and the EU and restoring value back to shareowners many of whom were left with very little as a consequence of the behaviour of the stewards of their capital. It is also about restoring the importance of values as a driver of business decisions that drive long-term reputation and in turn, long-term creation of value.

VALUE AND VALUES

Financial services in particular and much of business in general became obsessed in the 1990s with the concept of shareowner value. Championed by business academics[9] and sold in by smart US-based management consultants[10] the proposition was both simple and compelling: it is the owner that is the most important stakeholder and as such the owner needed to be confident that they were getting the best returns for their investment. Financial models were transferred from theoreticians in business school economics departments, through the trading floors where calculations were made on owner returns as a basis for making investment decisions into the management of the business. Organizations in every sector adopted the creed of 'Economic Profit' (EP) or 'Economic Value Added' (EVA) as the defining internal measure that best approximated to the assessment of returns made by a shareowner. Simply put, EP/EVA is the profit remaining in the business after taking into account the full cost of the capital employed within it. It is the ultimate test of whether your owners would have been better putting their money in the bank or in another alternative stock, the owners' return being defined as the rise in the share price over time plus the sum of the dividends paid out during the same period. This definition is important in that those who put their faith in this as the sole determinant of performance for a company argued that it was relative performance that drove investor decisions, i.e. an investor would always want to put their money where they could get above average returns. A well managed company would therefore always look to perform at least better than the average of the peer group. This economic thinking was then linked to classic business school strategy thinking, primarily that on competitive advantage, taken from Michael Porter's classic work *Competitive Advantage*. A model developed that used EP/EVA as a driver of resource allocation, financial and human, with a view to delivering 'above average' outcomes for the owner.

The driver for this movement came from a worthwhile concern that shareowners were not getting the most out of their investments in public companies through poor decisions made by executive directors and managers. Also, the stewards of the owners' investment were taking home rewards that failed to incentivize behaviour that aligned their activities with owners' interests and indeed often showed an inverse relationship to the value created for their owners. The Marakon model in particular demanded better strategic capabilities and clearer thinking in resource allocation from directors and managers. When it was linked to a programme of culture change it drove some significant improvements in performance over three to five-year periods. The outcome of its application, like any great theory, was patchy and failed to take full account of two aspects of human behaviour. The first is what drives investor behaviour. In an economics model an investor is always rational and will always look for the best returns because that is the only way any theoretical model can make sense. However, we know from Adam Smith's observations of Scottish investors[11] and indeed from other research on investor behaviour that there are several motivators for an investment decision other than 'best return' calculated using a complex mathematical equation.[12] The second is the behaviour implications of the application of 'above average performance' and therefore 'benchmarking' organizational performance, and even more importantly, senior executive reward outcomes, against a relative performance measure. Over the long term, the average return for the market as a whole is the best value the average investor can really hope for. Whilst in specific time periods the average investor may well get ahead through backing a particular sector or company, they are also equally likely to fall back through backing other far less successful ones. When stewards are asked to achieve 'above average' peer group performance the implications for sustainable long-term value creation are not necessarily positive. Making strategic decisions against a ranking target in a self-selected peer group has to run a strong risk of perverse actions to achieve yet another purely financial outcome (albeit driven from an external perspective rather than one based on internal accounting measures).

The largest element missing, however, from the EP/EVA proponents is the importance of the intangible concept of reputation, as discussed earlier. Economists dislike the intangible. It can't be measured and is often ignored (as in the concept of ceteris paribus) or given a constant value, but customers, consumers and suppliers can make decisions that have no regard to the returns being generated to the investor. Indeed regulators and legislators can often make decisions that fly in the face of the interests of the 'rational investor'. One apocryphal story comes to mind of the retail bank who applied the Marakon model to such a degree that in their call centres the call handlers were tasked to answer the highest value customer calls in the shortest time. Calls from low value customers were allowed to ring for far longer or even ring out. The assumption was that high value customers were important to the revenue generation of the bank: they had loans, higher mortgages, higher-value insurance products and at the very top end, significant equity portfolios. The economic value added of a single ordinary account holder was indeed far lower and theoretically therefore was an account on which one would spend far less time. However, the scale of losses of these account holders as they changed banks due to this poor service were such that the discriminatory call handling practice was soon discontinued. Indeed in the fifteen years since this story was told to me the whole proposition for UK retail banking has moved back from call centres where there wasn't a branch manager you could contact to personal bank managers available for extended hours including Saturdays. I bet this isn't the most efficient model in EP/EVA terms, but it is the one more likely to retain customers for the long term. This is all about values and how they are applied to your business.

However, in business appointments the identification of values, whilst as important to the future of the organization as value creation, is less easy to achieve. This is in part because it is very easy in a commercial environment to conflate values and value. Values define us as individuals. They shape our actions and reactions. They drive our view of the world and the solutions we choose to support to solve the problems we face. They are acquired as we develop as children and young adults. They don't often change that much and they rarely change radically. Hence the time it takes to move societal attitudes (which are the collective expression of individual attitudes which come from individual values). A value is a belief that is so central to who you are that it shapes your attitudes, your behaviour and your decisions.

Value and its creation is the bulwark of a free-market economy. Adam Smith argued in *The Wealth of Nations* that man was born to trade and that all voluntary exchanges increased prosperity. P. J. O'Rourke,[13] who revisited Smith's original treatise in his assessment of economic systems, *Eat the Rich*, described the creation of value thus:

> Wealth is created by any swap. It may seem like an even trade, but each trader gives up something he values less in order to receive something he values more. Hence the wealth of both traders grows. When Neolithic spear makers did business with Neolithic basket weavers, the spear makers were able to carry things around in a manner more convenient than skewering them on spear points, and the basket weavers were able to kill mastodons by a method more efficient than swatting them with baskets.

O'Rourke and those like him on the intellectual right have a habit of airbrushing out Smith's introduction of the notion of a social or collective perspective to activities within a market ('the guiding hand': the mechanism that described his experience of Scottish bankers of the 18th century in whom he observed a tendency to support projects and opportunities in Scotland or of benefit to Scotland even if they seemed to be proposing to create less value than other opportunities available). Nevertheless, they make an important point that the process of engaging in voluntary trading is instinctive in human beings. From trading collector cards in the school playground through swapping stamps to exchanging unwanted presents with your friends; even if money never changes hands, we put a 'value' on what we want and look for an exchange for it with someone who has an equal value for something we don't want.

As we traded more we developed money as an intermediary when the value exchange had to involve two or more transactions to create value for all involved. I use money in that I sell something to person A and then pay money to person B for the item of value to me. What is interesting, however, about the creation of value is that there is an unspoken assumption that both parties are acting in good faith. In a simple swap this faith is about the quality of the articles exchanged and their utility in the future. Where money gets involved it widens to include an assumption that the money is good (i.e. not counterfeit) and that the purchaser is good for the money.

Very early on markets proved themselves capable of behaving irrationally and being manipulated easily. Going back thousands of years there are stories in all traditions of fair and unfair exchanges, of rogue traders and of the unscrupulous use of false weights and measures or the dressing up of food and other basic requirements to hide rotting produce and poor workmanship. These early market failures were met by some of the earliest examples of state intervention and regulation and as trade extended outside of the immediate locality to activities that crossed borders so government established structures to ensure fair trade. The greatest example is probably Charlemagne (742–814) who left a legacy in Europe with a definition of weights and measures that standardized trade across the Holy Roman Empire and beyond, some of which (the monetary pound and the pound weight) last to this day.[14]

So the creation of value through the market mechanism requires some core values to be present for it to be effective. Without confidence and trust markets wouldn't work. If there is any doubt in this statement the digital age has presented us with one of the most transparent examples of their roles in the creation of value: eBay. In creating a virtual structure the developers of this online market place had to produce both the trading arena and the structures that surround it in such a way that buyers and sellers were prepared to trust it in their early encounters and that would build confidence in its efficacy as they continued to trade through it. Confidence-building attributes are detailed descriptors and the use of photographs to reassure prospective purchasers, reporting and sanction systems should unfair trading take place and secure payment systems. Trust-building measures are those that rate buyers and sellers through the eyes of those who have bought from them or sold to them. This virtual market demonstrates the role that trust and confidence play in underpinning the creation of value. It also shows us that in order to trade and create value most people in a market value honesty, integrity and reliability. As it is the behaviour of people in the market that determines whether it will create or destroy value and given that some people always behave badly it shows that the existence of a regulatory framework with sanctions is an important element of confidence building.

If the crash of 2008 has taught us anything it is not that the market system is wrong – we have not seen the triumph of socialism or of Marx despite the hopes of some on the left; nationalization of some assets was a reaction to market failure not an ideological proposition. It has reinforced the proposition that there is no such thing as 'perfect competition' and that markets unregulated and unconstrained are more likely to be distorted and ultimately become destructive. Our political leaders have been reminded that they have a role in regulation and intervention and it will be a very long time before any political party proposes deregulation as a serious policy option in the US or in the EU. The market is our only hope of surviving and thriving. For it to create real and sustainable value the market has to demonstrate that it is underpinned by strong values. For that we have to look to the leaders of those organizations in society who create value.

I started with the proposition that values are associated with individuals and that at a collective level values are an expression of those held by the majority of individuals in the collective. It follows therefore that organizations can have values, but only in that they reflect the majority attitudes and behaviours. As a result of this they attract congruent thinkers and can shape attitudes of those they employ. This is the basis of the work done on corporate cultures and illustrates the difficulty of changing cultures in organizations. There are many complex definitions of culture. However, I believe it can be boiled down to this: it is the way we do things around here. By this I mean that organization culture is the sum of the way every individual behaves every day. This is defined and established through leadership. In organizations it is leaders who set and shape the values and it is how they and those they employ behave that shapes our reactions to them. This explains why some leaders fail (their values do not correspond with those of the organization), why some organizations that need to change fail to do so (the challenge of changing the everyday behaviour of hundreds of thousands of people is too big) and why some organizations fail in their entirety (the accepted norms of behaviour undermine the creation of value).

In the public policy arena it is values that set the outcomes of individuals and organizations, be they political parties, charities or campaigns. In public policy, regardless of your political perspective, the aim is to act on behalf of the greater good. In private enterprise, by contrast, there can only be one leadership objective: that of maximizing the value of the enterprise for the benefit of the owners. However, it is the way in which the organization does this, the behaviours and attitudes that its leaders encourage and reward, that will shape long-term success. This success is built upon establishing and maintaining a positive reputation. Reputation lies at the heart of a successful enterprise and reputation is shaped by the reactions of consumers, suppliers, customers and the wider community to what the enterprise does and, even more importantly, how it does it.

There is a difference between acting as a corporate executive in a responsible corporation and acting as a developer of public policy. And we have to maintain this difference in a globalizing world. The activists and campaigners see people with power and believe they should use that power for the greater good, regardless of what the power they have is designed to achieve. They have in recent years lighted on large national and multinational corporations and have targeted them relentlessly to change what they do. They do this regardless of the economic consequences. If value is destroyed, so be it even if that value destruction is far more likely to harm a poor farmer say in Africa than it will aid the fight against global warming.

I believe they are doing this because of a failure of leadership in public policy.

No corporation I know is equipped, organized or has the capabilities to define the greater good, let alone a policy framework within which it should be developed. They will always rightly look to achieve an environment where they will create maximum value from their own perspective. Public policy leadership eschews sectional interest, champions the interests of the widest possible section of society and has to define the world in which the leaders of private enterprise can then operate and maximize value.

Whatever we as individuals want to see, be it a sustainable world, one focused on climate repair or one committed to relieve world poverty then those we must turn to are our political leaders, not those in charge of businesses, however large. What we should rightly expect of leaders in business is that they operate within the frameworks and laws set by our political leaders and that they always act with the interests of their owners as their paramount concern. Political leaders provide the vision and the frameworks in which wealth can be created and for what society should do with its share of that wealth.

The campaigners have to realize that the continuing global failure in public policy to set about repairing our climate, addressing the scourge of HIV/AIDS and addressing poverty at a time of unprecedented global wealth is a failure of political leadership and this vacuum can never be filled by chief executives. Unless we are prepared to advocate revolution, the world order will not change that much in the next twenty years. Some would argue that in these circumstances we have to hope that the choices made in unelected party caucuses, in ballot boxes, in board rooms and by ourselves as consumers are those that encourage authentic leaders to make the right choices not just for themselves and not just for their own countries or organizations but for the global community as a whole.

Leadership is all about being granted permission by others to lead their thinking – it is a bestowed moral authority which gives the right to organize and direct the efforts of others. In society today it is democratically bestowed, in history it was bestowed through heredity, revolution or coup d'etat. However it is given, it can be taken away – today mainly through the ballot box or through shareowner or stakeholder action and in the past through deposition, coup, revolution or immediate dismissal. Whatever the method, where those being led and those with an interest in effective leadership were dissatisfied, the moral authority was withdrawn and the leader was leader no more.

Moral authority does not come from managing people efficiently or effectively or communicating better or being able to motivate. You get moral authority by:

- Being authentic and genuine – believing in what you do, showing a willingness to be open to what you don't know and by expressing your true feelings and emotions.
- Demonstrating integrity – acting ethically, ensuring that your words and actions match; showing that you serve a purpose beyond yourself and through this you build trust.
- Having self-belief – being confident and showing conviction in what you do and how you do it; being able to articulate why your vision and your direction is right for the organization and those within it.
- Showing self-awareness – being sensitive to your impact on others and to the emotions and interests of others; recognizing when you are going too far or losing followers.
- Being able to demonstrate a real and deep understanding of the business you are in and through this build confidence.

We return once again to the importance of trust and confidence in leadership.

There is no doubt that the market can work to a social purpose better than any other form of economic system. I have no doubt that it is the system least likely to succumb to authoritarian and illiberal control and therefore be best positioned to enable people to achieve their legitimate aspirations. It will only do so, however, if it operates not just within strong and transparent global frameworks but also within domestic and international structures that are regulated and audited by government structures much closer to the operation of the enterprise.

Regardless of the public policy response, however, there is still a requirement for CEOs and boards to reassess what they do to develop, promote, support and challenge leaders and for potential leaders to ensure they have the right capabilities and values to succeed. This is about the trust agenda. Many of today's leaders have lost the trust of those whom they lead. They have done so through a failure of understanding that as leaders they can only really be effective if they retain the willingness of those whom they lead to follow them. It is the refusal to follow that deprives a politician of power, an evangelical preacher of their television audience and a CEO of investor support.

Leaders fail when they lose the moral authority to lead. They may not leave office for some time after they lose the moral authority, but they fail as a leader once this has gone. In business, in public service or in public life leaders lose moral authority for three reasons. Either they get found out through behaving unethically; or they become plagued by self-doubt and lose their conviction; or they are blinded by power and act in a way that divorces them from the values of those around them.

Having said all this, Hegel's argument still stands: you have to assume that, if someone has become a leader, at some point they understood the difference between right and wrong. It is up to them, however, at the end of the day to abide by a moral code. And it is up to us to ensure that the moment we suspect they don't, we do one of two things depending on where they are: fire them or vote them out.

Part Two

The Solutions

Chapter Five
The Manifesto for a More Authentic Business

Some two or so years after the global financial crisis and the revelations of excess at the top of some of the world's most powerful financial services organizations, it would seem that not much has changed in the fundamentals of how business leaders are doing business. Excessive rewards continue to dominate the headlines and there has been no systematic and comprehensive adjustment to reward expectations or mechanics at the top of big business. Even in banking where bonus systems have been reviewed, little in reality has changed for those in receipt of significant levels of personal reward. As North America and the EU make painful adjustments to public expenditure and as personal and corporate taxation rises in many countries those who received most and who continue to benefit most from state intervention to prop up the sector now complain most about the personal and organizational impact of clearing up the mess they got us into.[1]

Despite the words of contrition uttered after the collapse of some of the major banks and the near collapse of the system it would seem that business, and big business in particular, has learned little and has changed even less. If business is to re-build its reputation then there are actions to be taken not just by boards and executive committees but also by leaders in civil society. This book is not focused particularly on the public policy agenda, but there is a role for governments in working with business. The changes I am proposing can work to benefit all stakeholders, but only if legislators address some significant issues of public policy. The manifesto that follows addresses the changes to leaders and leadership thinking that has to happen in business if it is to be a positive force in the 21st century.

There is, however, a clear demand for political leadership in all countries to collaborate in changing the dynamics of the market economy. The collaborative approach here is important not just to deliver a better outcome for society as a whole but also for the current owners and employees of businesses today. If only some countries and economic groupings react then the endemic short-termism engendered by reward mechanics that drive business leaders will drive the wrong sort of change. We will see movements of capital ownership structures outside the well-regulated markets to jurisdictions where investor protection is less and where behaviour that destroys value finds no criticism or even exposure with far less onerous rules on disclosure.

Having said this, there is an overwhelming case in my view for a significant reform of corporate governance and ownership structures that can give the power back to the real owners of the capital employed in an enterprise. If we are to nourish and sustain the operation of a positive market economy then the public policy agenda needs to embrace the following:

- Promote civil ownership of capital, not social ownership. By this I mean that we have to recognize that the market is the most effective mechanicism for wealth creation for society as a whole. The state is the least effective owner of capital as it is not driven to ensure that the capital maximizes its return. What we need to do is to create ownership structures that give individual investors back their voice. We have to develop ways for people to translate savings into funds with economic influence which allows ordinary savers and investors to bring their interests and concerns to the fore. For example, by requiring fund managers to poll individual investors about policy positions on major investment decisions.

- Promote a share-owning democracy that ensures that all owners can influence outcomes, not just a few. Remove the rights of fund managers to vote on company resolutions without consultation with those whose money is invested in that fund. Impose the same requirements on banks and other financial advisors who operate as 'nominees' for the owner of the capital invested. Where pension funds are involved impose a requirement on trustee boards to agree their voting position not to abdicate it to fund managers and advisers. This becomes a critical duty of care where the fund manager, acting as an intermediating stakeholder, e.g. one who sits between the real owner of the capital and the managers of the enterprise, will benefit financially from the transaction under consideration. It is inappropriate and poor governance for a fund manager to cast votes from which they will benefit personally, with no supervision or oversight from those who own the capital.

- Reform reporting and audit. Make it wider than financial compliance and ensure that reports and accounts are transparent and enable all shareowners to make decisions with real information. Have one set of standards and take a stand to impose them through regulation with teeth. Make remuneration reports transparent, more detailed and make votes on them binding on the board rather than advisory. Adopt a compulsory reporting framework that covers more than the purely financial, informing owners and potential owners about the reputation of the company and, just as importantly, the trends in reputation as perceived by key stakeholders.

- Reform takeover rules to require organizations to gain approval of their own shareholders for takeovers as well as those of the target organization, regardless of the method of funding and regardless of domicile of the acquiring company. Review the treatment of debt funding for takeovers. For large multinational businesses try to harmonize taxation treatment such that business can no longer play one country off against another to grow profitability on the basis of taxation treatment, but ensure they focus on growing profitability by doing their core business as well as they can.

- Reform the process for the appointment of non-executive directors. We need to take away the role and influence of recruitment firms in the appointment of non-executive directors. We must oblige public companies whose share capital is available for the public to buy to advertise openly for non-executive positions. In this open recruitment process I believe there is a role for an independent agency, such as the UK's public appointments commission, to offer to firms and to individuals looking to offer themselves up as potential non-executive directors a pre-assessment process to judge overall suitability for a non-executive role. In the UK the government has already given a vetting role such as this to the Financial

Services Agency and its successor regulator after its abolition over the selection and appointment of non-executive directors in the banking sector. Larger organizations should be encouraged to consider reserving a non-executive position solely for smaller shareholders to ensure that the full range of owner interests is heard at the board table.

- Re-examine the rationale for and assess the impact of the introduction of the concept of the limited liability partnership (LLP). After twenty years there needs to be a full review of the use made by advisory firms of the LLP structures. How much have partners benefited from the taxation treatment? Has little or no liability changed the risk profile of the advice given and the behaviour adopted by advisors to the detriment of owners and other key stakeholders? In my view the LLP structure is an unnecessary additional risk in the business environment. LLPs should either remain as partnerships and return to being full entrepreneurs with the liabilities and rewards associated with high risk or they should be required to become corporations with all the requirements for disclosure and owner accountability that this brings.

- Finally, the G20 needs to come to a political consensus on the question of whether or not the question of size should apply just to banks or to all organizations regardless of industrial sector. Globalization creates opportunities for businesses and threats for citizens in equal measure. There are some sectors of the world economy where a few massive global organizations could potentially dictate to the market the terms on which they will trade and there are some activities where size and the distance between managers and activity is so great that major risks are unseen and potentially highly damaging: BP's oil drilling disaster in the Gulf of Mexico in 2010 is a powerful example of this, impacting on a major global economy and, even more adversely, on its shareowners.

These structural changes would help the owners of businesses regain control from management and would constrain risk and encourage greater innovation. They would also redress the balance of power between business and society.

If the 19th century was the age of political empire then the 20th century was the age of economic empire. The spawning of global, increasingly powerful organizations with an economic impact far greater than many nation states[2] and whose power and influence is often greater than the communities in which they operated has reached its apex. The 21st century will have to dismantle today's economic empires just as the 20th dismantled the political. We need to do this to protect investors just as much as we need to protect the communities within which big business operates. Thanks to BP, owners are now beginning to realize the downsides of infinite growth. When you become bigger than many nation states and as a result of that size fail to control your operations such that you inflict serious damage, then the value tied up in the organization can be destroyed as a consequence. The damage inflicted upon BP by the US administration will penalize hundreds of thousands of owners through lower investment fund returns and greater pension vulnerability as well as directly in reducing their capital. There has to be a size past which any organization cannot be allowed to expand for its own good, let alone to protect those whom it may well exploit unfairly. BP's CEO at the time of the Gulf of Mexico oil rig explosion, Tony Hayward, was the modern Ozymandias. In the eyes of many commentators he was too powerful, too rich and too divorced from the world to ensure that the values and safety first ethos his organization espoused were imposed every day throughout his global operations. He was also in my view the victim of the sheer size and complexity of the organization he was appointed to lead. His was not the only fault: BP's failure was the failure of many, including some other very large corporations. The multiple acquisitions of US companies (Sohio in 1987, Amoco in 1998 and Arco in 2000) on top of significant European additions in the same period (Burmah Castrol in the UK and Veba Oil in Germany) and the development of a Russian joint venture operation (TNK-BP) created a behemoth. These were huge challenges as growth of that scale through acquisition brings with it significant national and organizational cultural issues that have to be overcome. What seems clear even now in the near aftermath of the Gulf of Mexico disaster is that BP's management failed to effect the cultural changes required to impose a tight control on its operations. This is particularly alarming when one considers the discipline that any stakeholder would expect from a well managed organization that appreciated the operational risks of working in the petrochemical industry. I believe that BP will become the case study in what happens when you get too big. Size brings with it scale in risk just as much as in anything else. In the uncertain world we now live in one way to limit risk is to limit size and therefore increase control and transparency.

If society is to stay in control of the environment, scarce resources and the future, then we have to ensure that wealth-creating organizations stay at a size at which we can impose effective oversight and accountability. If we have a duty to protect the interests of owners as well as those of other stakeholders such as employees then we have a duty to ensure that our political leaders address these public policy issues. Let's hope that they are willing to do so in the face of opposition from the leaders of global businesses from whom they are only too willing to seek support for their domestic activities. Business as a source of funding for vanity projects such as the sponsorship of global sporting events; as the arbiters of investment decisions that create jobs for people from whom politicians want votes; and most directly of all as a source of funds for political careers is a feature of domestic politics in countries large and small. It is always tempting to conflate the proper governance of wealth creation with the potential benefits wealth can bring: for the sake of the reputation of both business and politics, it is an unwise temptation to which to succumb.

This second part of the book lays out a manifesto for a more authentic business model than that we see in many organizations across both the private and public sectors today. One that accepts the need for public policy frameworks such as that I have described and that requires a re-evaluation of leadership and the role of the leader. This is a major change programme and one that requires those who have to change the most to accept the need for change. I believe a public policy response that reconnects the real owners of the capital with the stewards of their investment would transform the conversations in most board rooms and in fund management organizations. Alignment with the real interests of real owners as opposed to the economic interests of investment fund managers looking to maximize their own compensation will be a major driver of accepting the need for change.

Once businesses accept they have to change, then I believe they need to look at changing their strategies and policies in three areas.

First and foremost we have to reassess and reposition the concept of 'talent'. Talent as a term needs to become inclusive rather than exclusive. It has to be about everyone in an organization, not just the few. It needs to help us understand how we harness the power of every employee, not just the super-powers of a few 'high flyers'. Secondly, we have to achieve a step change in senior executive remuneration and performance management. Neither owners nor society in general benefit from the creation of a class of super-rich whose wealth comes from their taking no personal financial risk, whose protection from the consequences of their actions is so complete that they cannot be dismissed without significant compensation and whose standing and network in their sector can almost always ensure that they can find another equally rewarding role regardless of their track record. Thirdly, we have to redefine what we mean by an effective leader and leadership. We need to change leadership education in business schools and elsewhere to accept that effective leadership is more important than the individual leader. The acceptance of a collaborative leadership model where the contribution of many is the creator of value and the end of the cult of the leader as hero and sole achiever is a prerequisite of the changes we want to see in the way we run things in many countries today. It goes against so much of how we were educated at school and what is reinforced as we enter the world of work, yet without changing this paradigm we are forever condemned to be at the mercy of the actions of the over mighty: be they in politics, in business or in charge of a vital public service. The next three chapters explore these themes in detail and lay out a manifesto for change.

Chapter Six
Diamonds on the Soles
of Your Shoes
The Real War for Talent

Paul Simon's lyrics from one of the big hits on his *Graceland* album have sparked a great debate about their meaning. The reference to diamonds is commonly thought to have come from an observation from the early days of the South African diamond mining industry where the prospectors walked around with tiny diamonds stuck into the mud on the soles of their boots seemingly unaware of the riches they literally have beneath them.[1] The perceived lack of understanding that this could be a source of wealth was seemingly inexplicable in the circumstances: and such is the attitude of those who bought the proposition that there was a 'war for talent'. Malcolm Gladwell is one of the most famous sceptics of the propositions behind the idea of a 'war for talent'. His challenge to the basic concepts saw the beginning of what is now a significant re-evaluation of the arguments first put forward by McKinsey & Co in the early 1990s that there was a shortage of people who could drive superior performance in business. The authors of the original paper and subsequent book argued that the organizations who would deliver the best results were those who attracted and retained these top performing people. The 2001 update of their original 1997 paper asserts:

Having great managerial talent has always been important, but now it is critical. In today's competitive knowledge-based world, the caliber of a company's talent increasingly determines success in the marketplace. At the same time, attracting and retaining great talent is becoming more difficult, as demand for highly skilled people outstrips supply.

The war for talent will persist for at least the next two decades. The forces that are causing it are deep and powerful. The war for talent is a business reality.[2]

McKinsey took this proposition and used a mix of demographic data and an assertion that those who excelled at talent management (as defined by them) had shareowner returns some 22 percentage points better than the average in their industry. This created a 'burning platform' that argued that employers had to identify their top talent and 'shower them with job opportunities and pay them for the value they created'. The methods for identifying what constituted top talent was based on arguments that were built on approaches developed initially in the 1940s by the UK's Royal Air Force in trying to understand how they could select the right young men to develop as senior officers in fighter squadrons at a crucial stage of the Second World War. This simply got senior officers to allocate more junior individuals into three buckets (A, B, C) based on some clear and relatively constrained measures associated with the skills required to shoot down enemy plans, avoid being shot down yourself and protecting the slower bomber transport from attack. The As were singled out for fast track promotion, the Bs were reinforced in the current roles and seen as longer term potential for development and the Cs were managed more closely and seen as candidates for further training to improve their performance in their current roles. McKinsey took this framework and transported it lock, stock and barrel into the modern corporation. Gladwell and others[3] have argued that there was a fundamental flaw in the transposition of these insights from a very particular set of circumstances to apply to a much more general principle and from a single gender focus to one across both men and women. For example, these critics have questioned whether tangible outcomes over relatively short periods of performance have any correlation with performance in a more senior role. They questioned whether recruiting people and promoting them because of their intellect has any merit given there is no basis in research to justify a correlation between IQ and performance and whether systems such as these merely reinforce corporate cultures, including those that are toxic. Whilst these may be seen as technical points they are nonetheless important in exposing the significant flaws in the 'research' that underpinned the proposition.

The ready acceptance of a flawed proposition by so much of business (and public sector) leadership is worthy of some exploration. First, as we've seen from the research on prevailing social attitudes, it played to many egos in a generation that was already prone to be egotistical. It explained why they were leaders and why they were special and why they deserved to be rewarded and retained. Secondly, however, it also exposed a fundamental weakness in their business and management education. Whilst McKinsey may have produced an hypothesis which became a business bestseller[4] they had not produced a well evidenced and supported thesis. The failure to appreciate that the difference between a proposition that speculates on an explanation for superior performance and a proven argument against which action should be taken is a vast gulf was a significant error. The failure to demand far greater empirical support, spurred on no doubt by the implied flattery to those it was pitched to at the top of big corporations, supported by the reputation of one of the big names in management consulting, has cost businesses and their owners dear.

So what do we really know about people and their capacity to perform? How should we utilize this knowledge to ensure that we build and develop the talents we already have in the organization? Enabling people to employ all their talent in the support of any organization seems to break down into three things: maximizing their innate skills and capabilities including intelligence; building their emotional commitment to the organization for which they work and creating a strong personal engagement with the organization. Get the right combination and people can deliver outstanding results regardless of role.

In an article for the *Ivey Business Journal*[5] I explored the linkages between commitment, engagement and success and argued that they were well evidenced. I firmly believe that this is the talent challenge facing leaders in modern organizations. Without engagement no organization can hope to align the efforts of its people with the goals it has set. Without alignment there is far less hope of successful execution of strategy. Ultimately it is the successful execution of strategy on which leaders must be judged. I believe this is the 'war for talent' that all organizations have to win: not to build a super-race, but to get the talent you have to realize that they can make a significant difference to the future.

The interactions with stakeholders such as consumers, suppliers, customers and communities are significant drivers of performance. So is the reputation that is established with regulators, policymakers and those who influence them in pressure groups. In a world where these stakeholders are just as likely to be thousands of miles away as they are to be next door, ensuring strategic alignment and a clear understanding of the rules of doing business are major challenges.

I believe that leadership at any level, from chief executive downwards, is about facing and resolving a series of dilemmas and when faced by a dilemma, as a leader you have to make a choice. A right choice requires good data, critical analysis, an understanding of goals and strategy, and an appreciation of the wider implications for the reputation of the organization. Disengaged people are far less likely to make right choices and ultimately are far more likely to make wrong choices which could, at the very worst, so badly damage reputation that it may never recover. This is a risk that no modern leader in any organization, voluntary, public or private sector, can ignore, hence it needing to be at the heart of any talent strategy.

Gallup[6], Sirota[7] and others have all done work which demonstrates the correlation between engagement and superior performance. They have also pinpointed an important distinction between commitment and engagement. Commitment is the emotional attachment one has to the organization within which one works and the pride one has in its achievements. It is driven by a personal association with positive values that are clear and adhered to, by an active engagement by the organization with the community and by a positive culture. Engagement, on the other hand, is more than commitment in that it is the demonstration of discretionary effort to ensure the organization achieves its goals. Discretionary effort not in terms of working long hours, but rather in terms of thinking more carefully about the organization as a whole before drawing up plans and acting upon them. It is driven not by the organization but by the experience of being managed within it on a day-to-day basis. The distinction here is important if one is to understand the role of leadership in an organization as opposed to that of management.

During my time at Cadbury Schweppes, we introduced a global climate survey which supported a significant cultural integration programme following the acquisition of Adams Inc, a global confectionary business based out of Parsippany, New Jersey. This survey was an integral part of a global programme of change that introduced a new business model, new operational models, new IT platforms and a restatement of the Cadbury Schweppes values and ways of working. It was designed to act as a catalyst for change at a local, regional or global level. It did this by providing the leaders in the business with a measure of the degree of commitment and of engagement at each of these levels. The purpose was to focus strategic management attention on what could drive improved business performance and where leaders might want to focus resources to achieve their goals. The actions that stemmed from it drove the Cadbury Schweppes talent management strategy which we saw as inclusive. Our strategy was to take the diametrically opposite position from that mapped out by McKinsey: every employee was to be treated the same.[8] We wanted every employee, regardless of level, not just to be committed to Cadbury Schweppes, be they from the original business or from the new acquired Adams

Inc. We also wanted to ensure that they were as engaged as we could make them, because without this engagement, we would fail to deliver the ambitious business goals we had announced on completion of the acquisition. Looking to build effective day-to-day people management at every level in the organization sat at the heart of our talent strategy. The 'war for talent' as far as we were concerned was all about maximizing the potential of what we had through building the highest levels of engagement we could.

As we worked with the first results and the people development plans that arose from local workshops we established two key insights which we believed sat at the heart of winning our 'talent war'. These insights also sharpened our understanding of the role of leaders in delivering the talent strategy. First, all our results, regardless of country, function or level of employee, showed a gap between the level of commitment in any organization and the level of engagement (commitment always being higher than engagement). We noticed that our superior performing organizations were those with smaller gaps.[9] This leads me to believe that the leadership agenda for talent, unless commitment is significantly lower than average for the sector, should be focused on how to close this gap. The other insight is about the nature of engagement itself in that whilst commitment can be influenced significantly, though not exclusively, by the leadership of an organization, engagement is primarily, though not exclusively, the outcome of the interaction between an individual employee and their line manager. At Cadbury Schweppes, we expressed this second insight in the following way: 'My line manager is the lens through which I look at the company, and through which the company looks at me.'

The leadership agenda for talent is therefore far less about what leaders can do directly (apart from when they are acting as a line manager themselves) and much more about what they have to get others to do; virtually always when they are not around to see it happen. So as a leader they need to be a role model of excellence in managing people and a champion of investing in the development of world class people management skills. This is the antithesis of the way the McKinsey 'talent myth' has been implemented in many global corporations.

In my mind too, this explains why so many organizations find it difficult to convert commitment into engagement. To do so requires that every line manager be able to impact positively on everyone who works for them. However, what is also true is that you can't have engagement without commitment. So, what do leaders have to ensure their line managers have to do effectively to maximize the talent available to them? David Sirota[10] posits that engagement is driven through three key factors: Equity, Achievement and Camaraderie. He defines equity as being treated justly in relation to the basic conditions of employment. The basic conditions are: physiological, such as having a safe working environment, a balanced workload and reasonably comfortable working conditions; economic, such as a reasonable degree of job security, satisfactory compensation and benefits; and psychological, such as being treated with respect, credible and consistent management and being able to get a fair hearing for complaints.

These are interesting in that they are pretty basic requirements, yet despite that, they can be radically affected by an individual line manager. Whether or not there is a respect for safety, whether one is treated as an adult rather than a child or an untrustworthy adolescent, and whether issues are dealt with fairly are all down to the individual. Even reward is ultimately an individual issue for many despite the fact that organizations have pay and benefits structures. Other research would add one further driver here with which I would concur: the proper handling of poor performance. For an individual, there is nothing more discouraging than working hard and watching others get away with far less. In fairness to McKinsey this was something they stressed in their model for building a 'talent' organization. However their focus was much more about not tolerating 'underperforming' leaders than address-ing and resolving performance problems and in the excessive way this was implemented in some organizations it was rapidly trans-lated into a policy of 'firing the bottom 10%'.[11]

Camaraderie is defined as having warm, interesting and co-operative relations with others in the workplace. Gallup[12] asks one single question in its survey to get at this: 'Do you have a best friend at work?' This may be for some a rather simplistic measure, but in my view, one of the largest differentiators in the UK's 'Sunday Times' 100 Top Companies survey is the pride and comfort employees have in the community that is the workplace. It is, after all, a basic human requirement to want to belong and to be accepted as belonging. Again, like in the other areas, so much of this can be determined by the behaviour and attitudes of the individual line manager.

If you dissect these empirical studies which cover many tens of thousands of employees, the same conclusions can be drawn: com-mitment is essential to drive engagement. It is based on working for a company of which one can be proud in terms of its core purpose, its ethical stance and its successes. Engagement, however, drives superior performance and it is down to how individuals are managed. What makes this even more challenging for today's leaders is the trends first identified in the mid 2000s that started to show the beginnings of some major changes in the nature and management of work. First, in the next twenty years there will be demographic changes in the structure of workforces in many developed and some developing economies. For example, there will be 10% more people in the UK workforce by 2025,[13] yet the economy is likely to grow roughly at the same pace over the next twenty years as it did in the previous 20, when 48% more people entered the UK workforce.[14] This can only exacerbate key skill shortages and continue to drive tensions about the nature and purpose of immigration.

Secondly the nature of the work itself will change with a growth in demand for what is being called 'social capital' skills – the ability to work collaboratively. Skills such as 'listening carefully to colleagues' will become central to work.[15] Thirdly, the dramatic changes in how people work today will accelerate even faster. Today, over 5 million people in the UK, almost one fifth of employees, spend some time working from home or on the move. Mobile workers are likely to become one of the fastest growing groups of employees and the way they are managed will have to change dramatically.[16] Fourthly, the nature of organizations could well change, with innovation being led from the most customer-facing of employees and managers no longer being the prime leaders of change. Rather, they will develop into the role of designing and coordinating networks which allow others to lead where they have expertise. Being a leader will be more about designing, managing and repairing such networks.[17]

With engagement a big driver of employee loyalty and retention, the demographic squeeze will play badly for those who can't gain commitment or engagement. Organizations where line managers behave in ways that create an engaged community are those that will find it easier to build 'social capital' and to work within a less rigid and hierarchical structure. Where your workforce is increasingly mobile, ensuring engagement is essential if they are to make the choices you want them to make when they are at a distance from the management structures within which they operate.

Ultimately, if the futurists are even half right, the 'war for talent' will be fundamentally about the importance of building engagement for successful performance. This is not the job of one leader, but of many leaders and all managers. What the research tells us is that the creation of an elite class of super-heroes treated completely differently from the mass of employees in the organization is unlikely to make any significant difference at all to the long-term value created for owners and wider society. In fact as we have seen from the many tales of corporate failure in the last twenty years, an elite, corrupted by power, distanced and distant from the mass is a sure sign of impending collapse. This shouldn't be new news, after all it is what happened in France in 1789 and in Russia in 1917 and again in 1992.

What it also tells us, however, is that building a detailed understanding of the potential of every employee, investing in it and ensuring it is well managed on a daily basis is far more likely to deliver consistent and sustainable superior performance. This is difficult and challenging to do; it has as much to do with the qualitative aspects of organization leadership as with the quantitative. It requires an organizational capability to make effective judgements about potential, investing in education, training and development, building cultures that attract people and make them want to stay and creating a management cadre that have the skills and the commitment to engage those who work for them. This in turn requires leaders who value the efforts of the whole, not just of the few.

The 'war for talent' proponents offered not just a flattering proposition that supported the significant hikes in senior executive remuneration and enabled the development of toxic cultures that reinforced senior leader prejudices and beliefs. Just as importantly it provided a rather lazy solution to business leaders who were unwilling or unable to take on this complexity: identify the top talent, invest in them and leave it to them to make a difference. I guess the one thing we can all agree on is that in financial services, in Enron and WorldCom and in many other active adopters of this philosophy, they certainly made a difference: not quite the one, however, McKinsey & Co predicted. The outcomes have been far less investment in building basic people management skills as resources went to 'high potential' and 'leader' development. Spiralling entry salaries at graduate and MBA levels created excessive expectations for these new entrants. Corrosive cultural differences between them and the majority of their less well treated colleagues and promotion pathways ensured that 'top talent' spent less and less time in any one job and as a consequence had far fewer opportunities to learn from their mistakes. Indeed these people moved so fast the only thing that stopped them was the mistake they made in the senior job from which they got fired.

This is not a manifesto for greater investment in the human resources function and the processes and bureaucracies they bring with it: far from it. Indeed one might argue that the enthusiastic adoption of the talent myth by HR professionals as a lever through which they could gain influence and credibility was one of the reasons it attracted so little in the way of rigorous review and challenge. It certainly enabled them to build an industry in assessment and development tools and techniques, 360 degree feedback surveys, capability and competency models and very expensive leadership development programmes with a penchant towards the exotic. Many major corporations invested significant sums in such activities only a few years later to throw out the models and processes that cost them so dear.

This is a manifesto that argues for making talent development a leadership priority not an organization process. By this I mean that leaders have to put in place a culture where people can explore their capabilities, identify how to maximize their impact and be supported through development to achieve their potential through delivering organization goals. If this sounds a little like motherhood and apple pie, there are plenty of great examples out there. Distilling them down suggests the following key principles need to be in place.

DEFINE AND COMMUNICATE A CLEAR CORE PURPOSE

People work best in organizations where there is a clear and commonly understood reason for that organization to exist and with which they can easily identify in their daily routine. In their book Jim Collins and Jerry Porras[18] lay out through examples across a number of sectors the importance of what they have defined as 'a core ideology' for the consistently effective performance of some of the world's leading firms. This provides an organization with a common purpose which they argue is something every employee can commit to and which helps guide decisions about priorities, resource allocation and people development. Importantly it is not a vision nor is it a mission statement: it explains why the organization exists. It reminds me as an employee why I come to work here and what collectively we are all trying to achieve. It is absolutely not a goal nor a measureable outcome or something to do with creating shareowner value. It is a motivating reason to stay and to ensure you try your best to ensure your work is done well. It is a core requirement I believe to build commitment and a prerequisite for creating an engaged workforce. It is also a powerful attractor of people. Interestingly, interviewed about the leadership lessons from his research for his book *Good to Great*, Collins made this observation:

> There is a direct relationship between the absence of celebrity and the presence of good-to-great results. Why? First, when you have a celebrity, the company turns into 'the one genius with 1000 helpers.' It creates a sense that the whole thing is really about the CEO. At a deeper level, we found that for leaders to make something great, their ambition has to be for the greatness of the work and the company, rather than for themselves.[19]

RECRUIT FOR ATTITUDE NOT SKILLS AND EXPERIENCE

This sounds counter intuitive and certainly flies in the face of much of the thinking that supports the talent myth.[20] However it seems clear that commitment and engagement come as much from the attitudes of people in the organization in that they are willing to work collaboratively and suborn their own ambitions to those of the group as they do from having leaders and managers with the right interpersonal skills. With the exception of professional qualification and accreditation requirements to undertake technical roles in areas such as medicine, architecture, law, accounting, etc., which are clearly prerequisites to perform to an approved standard, the right attitude will deliver far more than the perfect experience or what look like the right set of technical skills. Ideally we want all three, but people are rarely if ever the ideal fit initially and increasingly more and more employers are plumping for the person rather than the c.v. There are many proponents of this position for small companies with research now showing considerable shifts in employer thinking where a positive attitude enables skills to be acquired and is the differentiator between good and poor performance. Examples abound, particularly where immigration in Western Europe and North America has brought in new entrants to the labour pool with a strong work ethic. Those motivated to succeed in their new environment display an ability to transform their language skills rapidly to be able to progress through to more rewarding roles.[21] Research conducted in the US reinforces this from the opposite angle, showing that the contagion spread across a work group by one person expressing negative emotions was significant. A negative and uncommitted employee can impact group attitudes, structures and behaviour. Leaders looking to have a positive impact on the emotional environment, and use it to their advantage to drive change, should be aware that regardless of their efforts a corrosive employee can have a far greater impact:

> a situation in which emotions that may seem trivial to an outsider can greatly influence insiders due to a build up of continuously dealing with the other group members' emotion.[22]

In other words, small but continuously undermining behaviour that reflects a negative attitude to work, to workmates and to the purpose of the organization itself can over time have a significant impact on the performance of the organization as a whole.

This is not to undermine the importance of effective management and recognition of performance, but it can really only have a significant impact if it applies to committed people.

STOP LOOKING FOR GREENER GRASS

The problem with internal candidates, especially for promotion, is that we know their faults. The problem with external candidates is that we don't know theirs. The consequence of this is that more often than we think, the candidate we know least about is the one we appoint. What is particularly interesting about selections in these circumstances is the impact they seem to have on the organization itself. Research conducted in Australia suggests that where an internal candidate is appointed this is seen as being a better and fairer outcome as far as others already in the organization are concerned.[23] Other research suggests that far from there being the positive outcome often associated with justifications for going outside for senior roles there is evidence that demonstrates a negative relationship.[24]

There are always good reasons for doing either and individual circumstances must always drive the decision, but I think it is time we rejected the notion that a vacancy is always an opportunity to look outside for the best talent. More often than not perfectly able people, with the right attitudes and commitment, are available in your organization today. What they will need to succeed is support, space to develop and protection from the expectations of immediate over-performance. Instituting active regular reviews of potential successors is one way of building confidence across the organization for internal appointees, particularly if they have to be made across organizational boundaries instead of within them. Another is to adopt an open process of advertising vacancies within the organization, up to and including the most senior levels. Whilst there will always be reasons in an organization for treating an individual appointment as an exception and dealing with it on a confidential basis, it would suggest an unhealthy culture if every senior role had to be treated in the same way.

Finally, within the development process ensure that current employees are encouraged to express their long-term ambitions as well as their next move preference. Make it a focus of recognition of great line management to have investment in training, coaching and other development activity that supports the achievement of potential of a range of employees, not just the graduate fast-trackers.

HAVE A DEVELOPMENT AS WELL AS AN
EMPLOYMENT CONTRACT

We frame employment in terms of the obligations of the employer and employee through a very formal contract. In any jurisdiction the contract frames expectations and provides the point of reference for the resolution of any dispute. In many parts of the world it is as much a document to protect individual employee rights as one that lays out the rights of the employer. It is at heart, a quantitative document. It focuses on numbers and their relationships: hours of work, rates of pay, contributions to pension funds, duration of holidays, start and finish times, unsocial hours working compensation, notice periods, etc. What it cannot do, however, is to focus either party's attention on the quality of the relationship. It is the framework for a transaction: in return for the promise of labour, the employer promises an economic return. The contract is dominated by so called 'job dissatisfiers' or 'hygiene factors'. Identified by Herzberg in 1959 in a study that has never been contradicted these are one of two factors (the other being job satisfiers, or motivators) associated with successful performance in the job. In Herzberg's own words:

> The job satisfiers deal with the factors involved in doing the job, whereas the job dissatisfiers deal with the factors which define the job context.[25]

All a contract does then is to define the architecture within which the employment relationship will be conducted. It can never be a motivation, but it can become a source of dissatisfaction, particularly if one party believes it to have been breached by the other. If we consider the motivators identified in the Herzberg model they reflect many of the elements of 'engagement' described earlier:

- Achievement – the ability and the resources to achieve within the job.
- Recognition – regular and positive recognition from your line manager for achievement.
- Work itself – a satisfying role that provides sufficient variation and opportunity.
- Responsibility – the ability to take decisions required to do the job and to be given responsibility for goal delivery.
- Advancement – the opportunity to advance within the organization.

Herzberg's conclusions that salary is more of a hygiene factor than a motivator have been challenged from time to time, and were certainly rejected by the proponents of the talent myth, but they continue to be borne out by research. One example would be a survey by Development Dimensions International published in *The Times* in the UK. The survey in 2004 interviewed 1000 staff from companies employing more than 500 workers, and found many to be bored, lacking commitment and looking for a new job. Pay came fifth in the reasons people gave for leaving their jobs.

The main reasons were lack of stimulus in their jobs and no or little opportunity for advancement. Forty-three per cent left for better promotion chances, 28% for more challenging work; 23% for a more exciting place to work and 21% for more varied work.[26]

I believe that we should make these motivators just as important and give them just as much focus as the hygiene factors currently in the contract of employment. This could be addressed through the introduction of a 'Development Contract'. An employment contract is inevitably a document that is static rather than dynamic and rightly so as it forms the foundation for what is hopefully a long-term relationship. A development contract has the opportunity to be a living document, updated annually where the organization and the individual focus on longer term goals they both share and it could record personal progress and the activities that support it. The contract could be framed to identify changes to the job and the levels of responsibility and resources and time allocated that will be made by the organization to enable the individual to deliver their goals. Like a development review it might identify the things the employee does well and how these will be developed and used over the next year and it would be the ideal place to identify the employee's aspirations. Doing this would allow for a shared understanding of how these will be supported by the organization in activities such as coaching, mentoring and more formal training and, when appropriate, the identification of a new opportunity. Discussing this regularly would create a far more positive environment and relationship that the annual performance review. I would argue that it is more likely to drive a more engaged employee and therefore better performance. With any luck it ought to reduce unwanted turnover as well.

GET RID OF COMPETENCY ASSESSMENTS

This is contentious and many HR professionals and academics will produce endless research and justification for doing precisely the opposite, however I still think it needs doing. Not because there aren't things that from observations over time and critical incident type analysis one could identify which correlate with effective performance. The question we have to ask is: whilst they may correlate statistically, are they really the single defining factor that has any bearing on the outcome? This goes to the heart of my argument against the leader as 'hero' and the concept of a 'Mary Poppins Manager'. Understanding the behaviour, skills and knowledge that you need to achieve your goals and stay true to your values is an important ingredient of organization success. Driving them into performance and reward systems such that you create the foundations for a culture of compliance and a community of clones is the potential outcome of taking one insight on the conditions for success and using it to define a rigid framework for assessment of contribution.

Competency frameworks have no place in taking account of the circumstances in which individuals may have to work. An individual's contribution is shaped as much by the economic or social context, environmental pressures, combinations of skills and attitudes in a team or changes in organizational structures as it is by their innate skills. There is little or no flexibility in the structures used in organizations that recognize that these or any other factors could shape individual performance quite dramatically. An individual does not change overnight from being effective to less so in a particular aspect of their role; however circumstances around them could make them far less effective.

Used in assessment, they also impose a false imperative: to be consistently strong at everything. To be anything less is to fail in the eyes of the organization and, if you accept the organization's premise, in your eyes as well. A study conducted by the UK's Institute for Employment Studies in 1997 looked at the integration of competencies into performance reviews and concluded that if the outcome of the review was that it identified a training or development need to improve performance in the role then it had a negative impact on the reviewee. However, if it resulted in a pay increase for the reviewee then it had a positive impact.[27] This is unsurprising in itself but reinforces the impossibility of conducting a fair review against a competency framework where, given that we are all imperfect, an honest assessment would find areas of both strength and weakness. A healthy organization would accept these, celebrate them and ensure that teams were well balanced and leaders had around them people who compensated for the things they did less well. In many modern organizations, this is not what happens. The more senior you are, the fewer faults you can have, and if you have faults at all, these have to be 'acceptable' ones. In my experience as a line manager in major global organizations the most frequently cited acceptable faults that reviewees are willing to see on their performance reports would be phrases such as: 'needs to pay attention to detail' (translates as a strong strategic thinker whose big picture vision makes him/her high potential); 'doesn't tolerate fools gladly' (translates as very smart person with real intellectual ability) or 'is impatient with others' (translates as high drive achiever with ambition).

If we think about attitude, what we really want our line managers to look for is people acting with honesty and with integrity on behalf of themselves and the organization; working hard on the right things; having effective relationships with work colleagues and external contacts and being committed to delivering agreed goals. How they do this is far less important so long as it doesn't impact negatively on others. Managers need to reinforce the good when they see it and challenge the bad on the same basis. Over an agreed period the recognition and challenge need recording and where challenge outweighs recognition, action needs taking. This should be the basis for all performance review systems.

There is a role for competencies. They should describe the full range of skills and behaviours that the whole organization requires for it to be successful. In this role they would be less relevant to the individual and more relevant to those responsible for organization development as they would then define the diversity of people required to deliver success. Diversity in the workplace should be the acceptance of individualism. In the last ten years or so in many countries it has been hijacked to mean an understanding of the need to include groups who have been previously underrepresented. Whilst this is a laudable public policy ambition, for organizations it can set the wrong agenda. Gaining agreement that it takes a highly diverse set of individuals to create success and then looking to recruit this diversity would achieve the objectives of those who seek to address access to the workplace for underrepresented groups. Couple this with the principle that all leaders are imperfect and we can begin to create positive and enabling cultures rather than toxic and compliant ones. Understanding our imperfections enables better teams to be built around those of us who understand the role they have in delivering successful performance. Using competencies to understand the diversity required in any organization in terms of attitudes, skills and behaviours isn't a revolutionary idea, but doing so would revolutionize practice and performance.

THROW OUT OVER-ENGINEERED HR SYSTEMS

Underlying this critique has been one of the functions of Human Resources as it operates in so many global businesses today. It is susceptible to fads and fashion, constantly introduces over-engineered solutions to organization problems and owns the systems and processes that cause the most pain and create the least satisfaction. It is time that leaders took ownership of what HR functions do on behalf of their organizations and looked to challenge the way performance management, pay and benefits and resourcing is done on their behalf.

One of the biggest challenges in today's organization is managing your way through the noise associated with performance. Goals, objectives, measures, PIs, KPIs, balanced scorecards, risk registers and all the other paraphernalia of today's results-oriented cultures create huge amounts of activity, absorb significant resources and generate vast amounts of data. I am unsure, having worked with all these frameworks in my time, whether they really produce any better hard information against which actions can be taken to adjust resource allocation, refocus activity or reallocate time over and above monthly management accounts and simple tracker measures on brand, product and customer activity. Too many indicators frustrate, often contradict and can create uncertainty where experience and customer or consumer insight would naturally indicate a particular course of action. Where these get layered onto an already complex process for individual performance management the ability for employees to get detached from the strategy and purpose of the organization, especially a large one, is relatively easy.

I am not a believer in performance management systems. I am a believer in strong performance management by line managers.

There is a very important difference. Most performance management systems are introduced by HR because they don't trust line
managers to do the jobs properly. These systems are therefore for-
mulaic. They outline a flow of conversation which never happens
in any other interaction (i.e. one that is logical, rational and doesn't
move in reaction to anything that is said by either party) and one
that in the hands of an unconfident line manager becomes stilted,
impersonal and ultimately unauthentic. What they do is ensure
that all boxes can be ticked that need to be ticked and that HR can
report to the board that a target percentage of reviews has been
completed on time. Forget the fact that most of them are ineffec-
tual, dishonest and an experience of mutual pain and anxiety for
many of the participants.

If the organization has clear objectives then these should be
understood by all, and local team and individual objectives need
to be clearly linked to them. There should be a few key objectives
for a time period with simple, well understood measures over
which the team and individual have control. This is what should
drive performance related pay. After this all we need to know is
that they have been reviewed, a conversation has taken place on
performance and what actions have been agreed for the next period.
A simple email from both parties confirming this and the action
plan should be sufficient. We don't need a school report format
which takes us back to teacher/child relationships and quite often
reads like the reports we get about our own children ('Mary had a
good year this year'; 'Jacob made a committed effort to achieve his
objectives'; 'It was a shame Susan's illness kept her off work for
some months', etc.).

Removing the required paperwork and requiring the line manager to manage, rewarding them for doing it well, can transform performance and relationships at work. It could also remove several heads from your HR function, saving you money and a great deal of environmental damage from excess use of paper at the same time.

INVEST IN LINE MANAGERS

All of this part of the manifesto is about leaders recognizing the value and importance of their line managers. For too long now the cult of the leader has diverted investment, focus and support for line managers, yet as we have seen they are critical to delivering the organization's goals and long-term objectives. I think they are the people who day in and day out deliver on the core purpose of the organization. Where they are effective, they nurture your talent and develop it, where they are less so they squander it, letting it leave and move to your competitors. Organizations undermine these managers by letting them get squeezed between the top and the bottom. They do this by removing too many of them so that their spans of control are excessive, by plying additional tasks upon them alone reducing the time available for directing and developing their teams and by undermining their authority by communicating around them and not letting them have sufficient power to act, especially on poor performance and on issues of discipline.

A line manager's job is simple: deliver today through those you manage and deliver tomorrow through developing those you manage. Trained properly and measured and recognized appropriately the line manager is the pivotal role in any organization. Left to guess what we want and disempowered they can become organization permafrost and worse begin to undermine the enterprise through negativity and resistance to change.

My solution is simple: take most of the money you've been spending on high flyer development and put it into line manager training and recognition. The high flyers will get there because their line managers will do a brilliant job. Without the line managers doing such a job, the rest of the organization will become sclerotic and regardless of your high flyers, it will fail to perform. The talent you see in your organization today is a fraction of what you have. What you don't see are the diamonds on the soles of your shoes: your line managers are the only way you can pick up your organization's feet and see if anything glitters.

Chapter Seven
Moving From Warm Gestures to Cold Showers
A Reframing of Executive Reward

It was J. K. Galbraith in 1980 who famously analysed the compensation arrangements of chief executives in large US corporations by arguing that the higher up in corporations people rise the greater the say they have in setting their own remuneration:

> Compensation in the large corporation has become very generous. No-one can seriously pretend (although some do) that it depends on the scarcity and thus market price, of the talent involved. [...] The salary of the chief executive of the large market corporation is not a reward for achievement. It is frequently in the nature of a warm personal gesture by the individual to himself.[1]

In fairness to Galbraith his words did not fall on entirely deaf ears. Legislators in North America and in Europe throughout the 1980s and 1990s acted to address this issue of control and influence with significant regulatory intervention. If we took the UK as an example of the level and focus on activity then one might argue that the business community and the government have taken his challenge very seriously. In 1992 a review of non-executive governance by Sir Adrian Cadbury,[2] set up in the wake of corporate failures, including yet another banking collapse, laid down specific recommendations to improve oversight and better protect the interests of owners especially as far as financial controls and executive director remuneration were concerned. Further concerns on director remuneration led to the setting up of a follow-up review by Sir Richard Greenbury in 1995. This laid down greater specificity in four areas:

- The role of the Remuneration Committee in setting the remuneration packages for the CEO and other directors.
- The required level of disclosure needed by shareholders regarding details of directors' remuneration and whether there was a need to obtain shareholder approval.
- Specific guidelines for determining a remuneration policy for directors.
- Contracts and provisions binding the company to pay compensation to a director, particularly in the event of dismissal for unsatisfactory performance.

As in the Cadbury Code, the Greenbury Code recommended the establishment of a Remuneration Committee, comprising entirely of non-executive directors, to determine the executive remuneration. However, in terms of service contracts, Greenbury recommended a normal maximum notice period of twelve months rather than three years as suggested by Cadbury.[3] Greenbury's principles were the first to articulate the importance of avoiding excessive compensation and in taking account of the levels of pay in the rest of the company. Yet, remuneration levels continued to cause concern and as a result in 2002 the 'Say on Pay' legislation saw the introduction of separate remuneration reports that get discussed and voted upon at the AGM, although these are still advisory rather than mandatory. Further reports and revisions to the UK's code of practice followed on from another review by Sir Derek Higgs of the role of non-executive directors.[4]

The impact of this concern for shareowners, however, has been negligible, in fact worse than negligible: it has been negligent. At the time of Galbraith's writing a CEO in the United States was earning about forty-two times the average blue-collar worker's pay. By 2000 this multiple had increased to 531 times.[5] As we have seen in the McKinsey paper, the proponents of the talent myth argue that the driver of this significant increase was the improvement in the underlying performance of the firm. Their proposition is that talented leaders drive better performance. They argue that as this performance improvement was the responsibility of the leader and their senior leadership team it is therefore entirely right and proper that in return the senior team should share in the value accruing to shareowners for that growth.

Even if one accepts for a moment that this argument has any validity, research, done again in the US, shows a potentially different explanation for the significant increase in the ratio between senior executive pay and that for the average employee. It analysed the proportion of profits that were allocated to rewarding the top five executives in US public companies. The analysis indicates a doubling in the percentage of profits absorbed by the costs of their total compensation from 5% in the period 1993–1995 to nearly 10% in the period 2001–2003.[6] So these significant increases in the differentials may well have been generated by remuneration policy changes rather than any significant shift in performance. Regardless of performance what seems to have happened is that those in trusted stewardship positions have managed to extract nearly double their share of profitability from the owners of the business over a period of less than ten years. A study in the US found that the high level of increases in CEO pay did not reflect a similar story in corporate performance.[7] A follow up report a year later identified twelve US companies (including household names such as Dell, Ford and Wal-Mart) whose boards' compensation committees authorized a total of $1.26 billion in pay to their CEOs who presided over an aggregate loss of $330 billion in s hareholder value.[8] In simple terms, despite all the regulation, legislation and corporate governance codes that followed Galbraith's pithy observation, large company chief executives and their colleagues at the top have handed themselves one of the largest and warmest personal gestures using other people's money in business history. To find anything approaching this level of self-aggrandisement in North America and Western Europe we would have to look at the exploitation by the aristocracy of the distribution of land, titles and natural resource monopolies such as salt handed out by absolute monarchs in Europe of the 17th century.

As a seizure of economic power from the many to the few this has all the hallmarks of a coup. So how, in a democratic society, did they get away with it? As I have covered in Part One, I believe there were three main reasons: economic, social and structural. Economic because this happened in a period where the increase in dividend and capital values[9] created a benign environment where owner returns were at a historical high. Any additional value being diverted towards the stewards of what was rightly the owners' interest was far less likely to be questioned. Coupled with the rise in real estate asset values in North America and Western Europe over the same period and with the majority of people, especially the asset-owning classes, feeling relatively well off this was far less of an issue. Social, because the changes to societal values discussed earlier in the book created a legitimacy to aspire to significant levels of wealth through activities other than hard work, personal risk, persistence and exceptional abilities. Being in the right place at the right time became as important as anything else. Structural, because the ownership of corporations became disconnected from the stewards who manage their interests. The role of the agent in exercising the power of ownership on behalf of the owner is one that, as has been noted before, has a distorting impact on management decisions and behaviour.

The issue now is this: are the owners too late to reclaim the value that is rightfully theirs? At the heart of this lies the topic of pay for performance of both corporate executives and of the agents who act on behalf of the owners of the corporation. Both are driven to behave in specific ways by the structure of the remuneration policies that apply to senior executives in modern organizations and unless both change, the fundamental misalignment between rewards internally within the organization and between the owners and their stewards will remain.

But before I move to lay out a manifesto for change in this area, it is important to reflect on why this widening gap in reward relativity is something that business itself needs to address. There are after all many exponents of the unfettered 'free-market' who would challenge my underlying assumption that this is a problem. One of the great benefits of capitalism, they argue, is the mechanic of the market which ensures that any resource, human or otherwise, will establish its own price. If in a resource such as people, where there are alternatives (currently about 6 billion of them globally) that can enter the market at a lower price then the market will adjust price accordingly; if there are no alternatives then the price will remain high and could well go higher. This is the state of 'Perfect Competition', where an informed buyer and an informed seller meet to set a true price. This, however, is always an aspiration. The perfectly functioning free-market as described in this model does not exist. There is never a fully informed buyer or seller – hence the attraction of inside knowledge in a trading situation. All firms, economic theory teaches us, are constantly trying to undermine the market to reduce competition and drive up price and therefore profitability. They are looking to exist as one of an oligopoly where they can restrict price competition or even better to be the monopoly supplier and therefore set their own price. The only challenge in these situations is to ensure that demand continues for the product, which is of course the economic justification for sales and marketing investment even where there is very limited competition.

In the world of talent and knowledge, it isn't the supply side that is the problem: it is the attitude of the buyer, or the demand side. Large corporations limit their recruitment pools quite deliberately. Many have bought the talent myth that intellectual ability shapes success far more than anything else. They look only to recruit from top universities and business schools, turning away without any attention hundreds of thousands of people every year who could achieve great things for them.

The recruitment market for MBA graduates is a good example of the impact of this restrictive behaviour. The top business schools in *The Wall Street Journal* and *The Financial Times* MBA listings achieve their status through a comparative ranking process. This has as a prime driver the salaries their graduates can command three years after graduation and the relationship of this amount to their salary pre-entry. Until the last couple of years these graduates went to the top firms in financial services and consulting where the salaries are significantly higher than elsewhere. As these graduates become recruiters themselves they then reinforce the importance of a restricted pool from which to source new talent by returning to their schools for each new recruitment year. Given this, it is not in the interests of the school to ramp up the number of graduates each year – that way lies a reduction in exclusivity, access to top jobs and a consequent reduction in the price they can achieve for the MBA. So between top schools and the top paying recruiters an artificial barrier has been placed on the entry of more equally well qualified and capable resources into the market.

Great schools, with fewer alumni in these top firms and therefore far less ability to sway recruiter behaviour to look at their people as potential hires, rank further down the tables as a result of their graduates entering different recruitment markets and commanding radically different salary outcomes.[10] Once supply is restricted, price can only move in one direction and as that is at one of the key entry points for future top talent, then clearly it adds fuel to the fire that reward further up the hierarchy will have to increase as well.

The proponents of the talent myth ignored these demand side failures – probably because most of them came from the top schools themselves. They applied this theory of pricing of scarce resources to the concept of 'the knowledge worker' as the source of competitive advantage. First introduced by Peter Drucker in 1959[11] this idea described a new type of worker whose primary capability was to work with information or who created knowledge which had economic use for the organization. He did this to differentiate this type of work as equally important for creating value from that which had historically been seen as 'productive' such as a production or service worker. The linking of the economic concept of a 'scarce resource' to that of the importance of 'knowledge' created the economic argument used by the cheerleaders for the 'war' for talent. Their argument was based in neo-classical economic theory. There is a shortage of 'top talent' who possess the 'knowledge' that every organization needs. Owners of assets in short supply use their advantage (often supported through an oligopoly or monopoly position) to drive up the price. This economic model needs to be applied to the owners of this scarce knowledge and therefore organizations will need to ensure that their remuneration policies pay as much as they have to secure this scarce resource. So, the only solution was for firms to ensure that they recruited and retained these very rare and very talented people by offering 'top dollar' packages. The consequences of this are well understood across much of business where it competes for entry to management level roles in sectors with international or global markets. What has been less appreciated until very recently is that the application of the talent myth across the private sector has inflated the cost of public service delivery. As salaries for 'top talent' (perhaps better described as people at the top who self-defined as 'talent') increased in the private sector, so salaries moved at the top of the public sector. For example in the UK's public sector nearly 400 top earners enjoyed a pay increase of over 10% in the two years 2006–2008, around three times the earnings increase for the same period in the country as a whole. In addition the numbers of people earning over £1 million p.a. had moved from one to four over the same period. In June 2010 the government revealed that over 170 public servants earned more than the Prime Minister.

So the talent myth was then compounded by the inappropriate application of the economics of pricing a scarce resource to remuneration policies. This drove the development of the packages that have seen chief executives take home in one famous case the equivalent of $100,000 a day.[12] It is the structure of these packages and their claimed linkage to corporate and individual performance which have created such a disparity of outcomes. There is no doubt that leaders create vision and guide strategy, but the execution of that strategy falls to the many not to the few. It is the relative inequitable distribution of the benefit amongst people who could all equally well claim to have contributed great effort to what is after all a collective outcome that becomes such a corrosive factor in modern organizational culture.

The reason I believe there is a problem is not only the negative cultural impact, nor just because these packages deny the owners of businesses the full value to which they are entitled. Just as importantly they have created an increasingly sharp social divide in societies that have been carefully constructed on the principles of equality of opportunity and fairness. Regardless of what we do, where we live or how we have been educated we expect to be treated fairly and equitably. This is a social problem and one that has to be fixed if we are to sustain an open, democratic and stable society. The demonization of bankers in particular and business leaders in general does society no good. However, it will not cease until they accept that their pay needs to be fair relative to others within the organization they lead. If they fail to adjust their behaviour and expectations then societies may well turn on the wealth-creating sector and punish it in such a way that it fails to generate the wealth we need for the future. Without that wealth we will not be able to take on the economic, environmental and social challenges of the 21st century.

As a supporter of the market as the only proven means of wealth creation I believe that owners, executives and policy-makers could create better solutions that reward the genuinely innovative and creative, make capital ownership and investment an attractive and rewarding activity and help build a cohesive society. However, before looking at the potential solutions, we need to consider the elements of performance based pay in organizations and how they are put together.

SALARY

In a report published in 2010 the Chartered Institute of Personnel and Development stated that only 25% of organizations who responded to their Reward Survey considered their ability to pay as the prime determination of the level of salary for a role. Over 70% stated that they were determined against 'market rates.'[13] As an owner or a taxpayer this should strike an immediate alarm bell. Who defines and sets market rates? How are they determined? Who has the information and what degree of transparency exists for both buyer and seller? With the decline in North America and in the UK (and indeed in the EU although this is less marked) of trade union influence in the setting of management and administrative salary rates we have thankfully moved away from the 'across the board' mentality of paying everyone on the same job the same total reward. However, what we have replaced it with is as inefficient. A system where salaries are often unadvertised, salary ranges often unknown to most staff and salary policies which are about relative positioning against a self-selected target group of peer companies with little or no link to affordability and company performance. The move towards this 'market-based' approach to reward has seen the emergence of an industry whose job is to protect organizations from exposing their pay rates to the market whilst allowing them to get a sense of their rates against those in the market: the remuneration consultant.

Remuneration consultants make their money through advising you what you have to spend to remain 'competitive' in the recruitment and retention of staff and in what ratio of say, fixed to variable pay, what level of bonus, pension contribution and other aspects of compensation. They all run 'salary clubs', made up of their clients (so automatically offering a restricted view of the market). Acting as honest broker they work with organizations to complete returns of actual rewards paid to people in particular roles, normally those for which they are most often in the external market place. What you receive as a compensation manager inside a large corporation is a report placing your outcome in a peer ranking. Using this data you can propose adjustments to current or future hire packages. No data, however, is provided with regard to such important elements as how did those who were paid more perform, individually or corporately? In the sector in which higher rewarded competitors are reported did something structural happen such as deregulation? Is this data skewed by a new external hire under pressure where a decision to pay 'what it takes' overruled a market-based assessment?

If this is the rather sub-standard information supplied to large organizations on which they take decisions, just think about small and medium-sized organizations who cannot afford to retain such an activity as a service. Often, they will rely on recruitment consultants who, not unreasonably if they are working on a percentage of salary as a fee mechanism, are likely to argue for a higher figure quoting jobs recently placed in the market. Even if they are on a flat fee linked to success, the higher the salary range, the greater the chance of ensuring that the full fee comes in quickly. On the supply side, real information is even harder to come by. Job advertisements at manager level and above rarely carry salaries in the private sector and increasingly fail to do so in parts of the public and voluntary sector as well. Your colleagues and your friends are a source: although I rather think the incidence of people actually earning more than you will correlate well with the incidence of those friends you had as a teenager who were actually having sex, as opposed to those who just liked you to think they were.

The one area where management salaries are clearly available in many countries is in the graduate-level entry market where on-campus recruitment and online marketing clearly marks out the initial rewards on offer. Here one can see in which sectors the talent myth proponents have really made their impact. For example in the UK entry salaries in 2010 were ranging between £15,000–£60,000 per annum.[14] It is no surprise to see the banks, the advisory firms and the consultancies paying the most.

Salary reviews in organizations take two forms: a cost of living adjustment often associated with national or regional rates of cost of living inflation and an adjustment that reflects personal performance, sometimes referred to as a merit review. In the private sector they are often combined into one single increase, whilst in the public sector, especially where there is a strong trade union influence, they are more likely to be separated. In the public sector merit reviews are still not available for the majority of management staff. They are often replaced by what is called a grade 'increment': a standardized increase that normally automatically applies unless the individual is in some form of 'poor performance' process or is under notice of termination of contract. This is the reverse of an incentive to out-perform others, rather encouraging people to do just what is sufficient to stay in the role for a guaranteed increase. In recent years this has often been worth much more than the cost of living adjustment due to low levels of inflation.

Merit reviews are more often than not driven by some form of performance review system which will summarize an individual's contribution into some form of overall grade. Many organizations choose to force the distribution of grades believing that regardless of the overall level of contribution it is still possible to identify a bottom and top 10–15% whose salary levels should be adjusted (or not) accordingly. The problem with this approach is twofold: first, that the overall assessment, whilst mostly supervised and agreed by a more senior manager, is a personal assessment by a line manager and there is little if any really objective application of criteria. Additionally, in a team where everyone has contributed equally well it is completely demotivating to be identified as a 'poorer' performer than your colleagues.

VARIABLE CASH PAYMENTS

Bonuses, incentive schemes and other variable reward structures are increasingly standard in all organizations. In the UK in 2010 over 70% of employers from all sectors indicated that such schemes existed in their organizations (with nearly 50% of public sector employers saying they now had them).[15] It is increasingly rare to find management jobs, especially at the senior end, with no variable element of cash reward. There is a difference here between jobs with a bonus and jobs with incentives that are designed to achieve a specific level of performance. In the job advertisements normally for roles with a sales responsibility you will often see reference to 'on target earnings'. This indicates a job where there is a low guaranteed monthly salary and an incentive scheme where payments will be made against very specific targets. Achieve the full target and the 'market rate' for the job can be achieved. Do better and you can earn more, do worse and your payment won't be as good as you had hoped for. This is the nearest you get in organizations to a purist form of 'pay for performance'. The other version of a variable pay scheme provides a bonus opportunity on top of the expected market rate, the payment of which may well be triggered by events outside one's direct control such as meeting a corporate profit goal. Here the salary reflects the 'market rate' and the bonus opportunity is used to recognize the stretch put into business plans aimed at driving superior performance.

Most management schemes are versions of the bonus model rather than the incentive one and are associated with a quantitative target (sales, revenue, profits being the most often used). Some will have qualitative elements such as achievement of personal objectives. The key issue with such plans is how you stop bonus payments to individuals when the business as a whole underperforms. Increasingly businesses set a corporate performance threshold below which no payouts to any individual will be made regardless of their personal contribution. Whilst this is increasingly standard practice in major corporations many are very sophisticated in setting the 'corporate entity', allowing the better performing parts of the organization scope for rewarding high performance even if the business as a whole has failed to meet owner expectations. The problem for the owner with these schemes is balancing the need to recognize high achievement in a particular area with the overall poor performance of the whole where returns are depressed.

There is no doubt that whilst individualizing salaries can be invidious, this aspect of cash reward can be developed into an effective reward and recognition mechanism, subject to the organization ensuring that the criteria against which payment will be made are strongly aligned to its overall strategy and purpose. The issue with bonuses as exposed by the practice in the banking sector is the value at stake and the short-term nature of the required periodic financial reporting process (annual in Europe, quarterly in North America) as good corporate governance.

SHARE SCHEMES

Many organizations run schemes that enable employees to acquire shares as part of their reward package. There is a continuum of ways of acquiring capital in an organization of which you are not the owner. They will range from the owner giving you stock from that which they currently own themselves, through the owner subsidizing part of the purchase price to enable you to buy more stock than you could on the open market, to the owner taking out options on the future value of shares in the business and awarding these to you, normally after a period of time and then only if the business has met agreed performance criteria. This latter method is the system still used by the majority of global businesses to reward and retain senior managers and executives. It is this system that has come in for the most significant criticism over the last ten to fifteen years.

Stock options are controversial for two reasons, mathematics and funding. Owners have significant degrees of discomfort with the theoretical mathematical base that remuneration consultants use to price the option to purchase. This is known as the 'Black-Scholes' pricing method. This calculates the expected benefit from acquiring the stock outright, sets this against the present value of paying the exercise price (normally the price of the stock on the day the option to purchase in the future is acquired) on the expiration day (normally ten years to the day after the option is acquired) and comes up with a fair market value of the end benefit (i.e. the potential value gained if the stock is sold at the end of ten years if it behaves in a manner similar to the assumptions in the model).

The model is fearsomely complex (as you would expect from a Nobel Prize winner in economics) (see Figure 7.1).[16]

The Model:

$C = SN(d_1) - Ke^{(-rt)}N(d_2)$
C = Theoretical call premium
S = Current stock price
t = time until option expiration
K = option striking price
r = risk-free interest rate
N = Cumulative standard normal distribution
e = exponential term (2.7183)

$$d_1 = \frac{\ln(S / K) + \left(r + \frac{s^2}{2}\right)t}{s\sqrt{t}}$$

$d_2 = d_1 - s\sqrt{t}$
s = standard deviation of stock returns
ln = natural logarithm

Figure 7.1   The Black-Scholes Model for Option Pricing

P. J. O'Rourke[17] laid down an interpretation (see Figure 7.2) of Myron. S. Scholes's later work on derivative pricing based on the same equation as follows:

Where C, S, N, 1n and K = things you don't understand
And r, s, t and e = things you don't want to know

Figure 7.2   P. J. O'Rourke's explanation of Option Pricing

I suspect O'Rourke's interpretation is the one most owners would go with. So if the maths is too complex for owners and indeed the vast majority of executives to understand, does it still work? Well as far as pricing options in an open market are concerned it continues to have a high degree of market acceptance as there is a built in assumption of the availability of what economists call 'assymetrical information'. In other words, the price assumption of the end value of the stock is calculated by people who know something, but not everything. There is an element of risk and if their knowledge is better than the average person in the market they can price better and increase their potential gain.

The issue is the way in which corporations use this market-based model to apply to an internal decision. They base their assessments on far more information than that which is available externally. In other words their 'assymetrical' advantage far outweighs the assumptions in the model. This allows them to model all sorts of outcomes to ensure that their top performing executives get as generous an opportunity as possible. They do this by looking for the values they ascribe to the variables in the calculation to create a reward that is as generous as they want it to be in terms of the multiple of annual salary that will eventually appear. In addition, they also propose what are called 'vesting' criteria: the performance in cash, profit, share price growth or related measure that needs to be achieved for their executives to be able to exercise their option to purchase the shares. These too are carefully managed to create the greatest possible chance of there being a reward. Recently, shareowners are becoming far more challenging of these types of schemes, but they still exist and they still get approved.

If the maths is one problem, the funding arrangements to enable executives to purchase capital and benefit from the gain in the share price over time are another. Large corporations create facilities using their in-house brokers and banks to enable executives to borrow money to execute immediate buy and sell transactions. This facilitates sometimes significant capital acquisition and disposal with no risk to the individual and, commission apart, no cost to the individual for the use of capital. Options are held after vesting at no cost to the individual either up to the date of expiry which, if an option vests after three years could mean another seven. The hidden benefits of these types of funding arrangements are substantial. None of these arrangements is directed at encouraging long-term capital ownership and given that executives are unlikely to have any significant personal capital to begin with they face no risk, nor any real negative incentive to think about long-term value. Where they can gain is to drive share price values artificially high to ensure maximum financial gain from a single transaction that sees them out of the market safely before the price falls.

Some corporations have responded in part to criticisms of options schemes putting in place shareholding requirements for senior executives. However, they haven't really addressed the fundamental issue: the failure of such schemes to expose senior executives to the downside risk of investing the capital that they have accrued over time. So whilst they can get all the benefits of ownership, they take none of the risks.

RETIREMENT SCHEMES

We are apt to forget that in Europe in particular, retirement investment schemes play a significant part in executive reward. Schemes
associated with supporting employee saving to fund their
retirement have formed a standard part of remuneration policies
at some levels in the organization since the early years of the last
century. All-employee schemes have been the normal expectation
since the end of the Second World War. In Europe the level of the
end benefit has been generous: in the UK it has historically been
around two thirds of one's final salary paid as a pension for life for
someone with forty years' membership of a scheme. The cost to
companies of these schemes has been driven higher by salary inflation, rapidly increasing longevity of their employees and in recent
years the failure of the capital and real estate markets to deliver the
level of asset growth required to keep up with rising liabilities.
Whilst it is true that these final salary schemes are less and less
common as the world recovers from the global financial crisis, they
have been replaced by schemes that will still create long-term liabilities for shareowners and that will still require a corporate
contribution. These new schemes, called 'defined contribution'
schemes, are much more similar to those available in the US enabling payment into a fund with no guarantee of the ultimate benefit.
Meanwhile at the top of organizations for some time will be people
who are members of schemes now closed to new entrants but still
requiring the corporation to fund benefits associated with more
generous times. The value of these 'pension pots' is increasingly
an issue for owners and policy-makers alike. Pensions are not
capped and are based on a final salary, rather than say a career
average. This can mean that senior executive pensions can be six

or even seven figure sums with the bulk of the funding having come from the corporation with the obligation to make up fund deficits falling on the corporation and any remaining active members (i.e. anyone still making contributions) of the fund. Pension fund deficits are now significant issues for owners and for potential investors with some funds now starting to freeze benefits.[18]

BENEFITS

Remuneration policies in large corporations still offer major benefits. Whilst these are now more transparent to the tax authorities than they used to be, they are often not as transparent to the owners: health care, cars (or equivalent cash payments), financial planning and tax advice are good examples. Whilst all employees can normally access discounted products and services where they work, quite often these arrangements are far more generous towards the top. Additionally, expenses policies seem to be ever more elastic, the nearer the top you go. At the most extreme, the stories emanating from the Lehman Brothers debacle, from Enron, from Worldcom and many others illustrate how large corporations now fund the personal as well as professional lives of their senior executives. The personal interests of senior executives seem to link to professional activities such as corporate support of the opera, theatre or ballet and entertaining your friends who, of course, are all fellow senior professionals. It becomes a business activity rather than a personal one where, to ease the intrusion of work into private time, partners are invited.

OPPORTUNITIES FOR CHANGE

This manifesto argues for root and branch reform of all these practices. The job of the wealth creating sector is not to fund the 'lavish lifestyles' of the senior cadre of executives responsible for its stewardship. Its role is to provide returns for its owners and in so doing to provide jobs for members of the communities in which it operates, customers for the smaller businesses who supply it and revenues to society through corporate taxes that go to reinforce the healthcare, education and infrastructure the sector needs to succeed. This is good business.

To achieve this change we have to put all these warm personal gestures under a very cold shower and to argue for a significant transformation in the way executives are recognized and remunerated for their work. Overall, we have to be prepared to set a standard that well managed businesses will follow. This has to include a mechanism that restores the relative rewards for senior executives against all other employees to a level that has broad social acceptance. Addressing the following would go a long way towards a much more sustainable framework for rewards.

CHANGE THE ROLE AND VISIBILITY OF SALARY

A salary should be the price that an employer is willing to pay for the effective performance of a set of activities which have been grouped together into a job. Your salary should be what you expect to receive for being good at your job. It should be very similar to that received by everyone else in a similar job in your organization. There is little to gain and much to be lost through justifying significant salary differences on personal performance and contribution because ultimately it is very subjective. This differentiation should come from variable pay. This salary should reflect affordability and should not come with any guarantee of any annual uplift. In a low inflation economy there is no requirement to increase salary every year and no good reason to increase fixed costs when there is price pressure that constrains your ability to recover these costs from consumers. Organizations should have a periodic review of salary positioning in the market, affordability and the position of employee earnings against the cost of living. However, if inflation continues as it has for the last few years then this could easily be biennial if not longer. At executive levels where earnings are significantly higher than the average the automatic annual review should end.

There is an argument for some level of explainable and understandable differentiation. Effective performance rarely comes immediately in any role and experience, appropriately utilized, can play a positive part. Salary bands have a role, therefore, but should be far less elastic than they are in most organizations today, with perhaps a 5% lower than target salary for new starters and a 5% greater then target for the most experienced effective performers. A simple mechanism for moving up these scales could be peer review, as opposed to management halo which is a prime mover today. Perhaps every two years with those whom peers believe are effective moving up perhaps 2.5% at each review giving a minimum of eight years in a role before one reached a maximum level.

There should be the same degree of transparency in the private sector as is imposed on senior executives and managers in the public sector. All salary bands and actual salaries should be clearly accessible internally and externally. The more owners have information through which to challenge and hold management to account, the more management will think carefully about the consequences of their actions.

USE VARIABLE REWARDS TO REFLECT PERFORMANCE

Whilst salary is a price for a role, variable pay in the form of an incentive or a bonus is the most effective way of recognizing and rewarding good performance. What gets in the way of effective use of such schemes is the imposition of an artificial period of measurement called 'the financial year'. For senior executives, the only measures that make any sense are those key performance indicators that are accepted by the owners of the business as the drivers of success for the long term. Increasingly, those associated with performance in areas not just associated with profits and cash generation but in what has come to be described as the 'triple bottom line' (where organizations take account of the environmental and social impact of their operations as well as the financial) have been used by investors and others as determinants of whether or not to buy shares or, for example, be accepted as a supplier for government contracts. These latter measures are inevitably longer term and the only way of being confident that financial performance has not been engineered by the finance function is to look over several financial reporting periods.

Incentive plans should therefore be longer term, linked to a range of measures and there is a strong argument to make these collective rather than individual. Research tells us that keeping criteria objective rather than subjective is critical in keeping people motivated and engaged. Differentiating between individuals in the same team as to the relative merits of their contribution just drives dysfunctional behaviour and builds toxic cultures. Differentiating between teams is much more straightforward and drives collective accountability and greater collaboration. The opportunity for personal differentiation would be to impose a clear and transparent mechanism to reduce the value of an award or remove it altogether where someone is under a poor performance review, or where identifiable actions have broken a code of conduct or where reliable employee feedback is negative.

Organizations, especially recently in financial services, have introduced one or another form of bonus banking where only part of a bonus is paid out in cash at the time of award, the remainder being held back for release over the following years in the form of cash or shares. This banking principle is sound and also has the advantage of smoothing out the impact of specific period performance, good or bad. It should become common practice with the caveats that (a) the retained amount should be no less than 50% of the cash award made; (b) all retained awards are used to purchase shares at the price in the market on the day of the award: the amount paid by the employee must cover the cost of the purchase transaction; (c) that no more than 20% of the shares in the bank can be sold in any one year; (d) bank values are transferable to new employers; and (e) the banked capital can only be released in full to the individual on reaching state retirement age.

Thinking hard about Greenbury's exhortation to avoid excess, no variable pay scheme should be able to award more than 200% of annual salary in any single financial year.

ABOLISH SHARE OPTIONS

Share options make business look dishonest. Even if they are genuinely tough and would only pay out if there were significant shareowner benefits, they are too complex, too open to manipulation, too able to be influenced by external events (such as a takeover for example) and too easy to take into account in tempting executives to move companies where there is no guarantee of any value being generated in the current employment. Sensible share programmes that incentivize long-term thinking and retain senior people who perform well in their roles are simple. They are open to a very small number of senior people. They involve allocating shares bought on the open market to individuals and do not release them until collective and/or individual performance criteria have been achieved. They should never involve a value of more than 100% of annual salary at date of allocation and their release should be controlled by the remuneration committee of the board.

REMOVE UNNECESSARY BENEFITS AND IMPOSE MUCH STRICTER EXPENSE REGIMES

Owners have the right to demand that benefits paid are strictly required for the smooth operation of the business. Health insurance for the employee, fine: for their family? Really? Why can't they pay? In a world where we all accept that cars contribute to global warming why is anyone offering them or a cash equivalent? If business acts together in these areas then no-one retains a possible competitive advantage in the recruitment market. There is obviously a difference in countries such as the US where the level and quality of free public health provision is very different from that in Europe and the pressure to have whole family health insurance is far greater. However, even in these circumstances owners must then be able to offset these with reductions in the value of other benefits. There is no automatic right to this at any cost without adjustment elsewhere.

On expenses it is time that non-executives acted to get the executive under control. Here the public sector in many EU countries and in North America set a much better example in their approach to using other people's money and the associated scrutiny that accompanies such expenditure. In business there is too much complicity and, at the margins, real dishonesty in the setting and auditing of expenses at the most senior levels. Having worked myself in both sectors it is my view that the taxpayer in the UK gets better value from expenses than the shareowner and this has to change.

CAP EARNINGS POTENTIAL BY INTRODUCING A RELATIVITY PRINCIPLE

The total cost of employment of a senior executive is significant and owners of publicly listed companies should insist that it is this total cost that is reported on at all levels in the business. It should be constrained by agreeing on a principle that the highest paid executive should never earn more than an agreed multiple of earnings relative to either the lowest paid or to the average employee. The UK mutual retail store John Lewis operated under a policy which defined a relative difference between the CEO and the lowest paid at twenty times. In more recent years this has changed to a multiple significantly more than double this original figure, mainly as a result of the moves in remuneration levels at the top of other retailers. Whilst having any cap may seem difficult for global businesses which do compete in very challenging markets, given the failure to adhere to the Greenbury principles of relativity to the rest of the company and avoiding of excess without a cap, then one should be actively considered. The range would have to be from between twenty to sixty times the average pay in the organization excluding the chief executive and his or her direct reports. Public sentiment would want to see something approaching the lower limit. If we chose the mid point it would take account of sector-specific recruitment markets yet still set something I believe society would accept as a relative difference. What this would do would be to act as a moderator on any cash bonuses paid out at the very top and along with the bonus banking would begin to rein in the culture of excess.

CHANGE THE REWARD STRUCTURES FOR
FUND MANAGERS

Fund management companies are generally paid on the basis of receiving a management fee equal to a certain percentage of the assets under their control. In other words they are paid for quantity as opposed to quality. Even if they lose you value as an investor in their fund(s), they will still expect to receive a fee. They recognize that the fee may well be less as your asset value has gone down so they work hard to gather in as many assets as they can to retain and increase their revenues.

To do this they look to back shares that are on the rise and to sell those in decline, primarily to ensure that their benchmark performance is above the 'average' of whatever peer group or target index they use to measure their success and attract new funds. The model of the industry as a whole fails to promote active and involved ownership, looking more for short-term gains to achieve performance targets just as do the executives in the companies whose shares they own. The industry model needs to shift from management fee to pay for performance. The fund manager must have their performance assessed in two dimensions, the financial and their ability to act effectively on behalf of the owners of the capital they manage.

RECONSIDER THE LINK BETWEEN MOTIVATION AND MONEY

Behavioural economists have been arguing for some time that the neo-classical economic assumptions about human beings acting rationally in their self-interest are beset by real shortcomings. Many of the models I have questioned in this book are based on this assumption. They believe that the neo-classical assumptions on human behaviour are not justified when one takes a human biology or psychological perspective of behaviour. In a guide to the principles[19] behind this argument, proponents of this perspective lay out seven principles that we should take into account when thinking about how people will act:

1. **Other people's behaviour matters:** people do many things by observing others and copying; people are encouraged to continue to do things when they feel other people approve of their behaviour.

2. **Habits are important:** people do many things without consciously thinking about them. These habits are hard to change – even though people might want to change their behaviour, it is not easy for them.

3. **People are motivated to 'do the right thing':** there are cases where money is de-motivating as it undermines people's intrinsic motivation; for example, you would quickly stop inviting friends to dinner if they insisted on paying you.

4. **People's self-expectations influence how they behave:** they want their actions to be in line with their values and their commitments.

5. **People are loss-averse** and hang on to what they consider 'theirs.'

6. **People are bad at computation when making decisions:** they put undue weight on recent events and too little on far-off ones; they cannot calculate probabilities well and worry too much about unlikely events; and they are strongly influenced by how the problem/information is presented to them.

7. **People need to feel involved and effective to make a change:** just giving people the incentives and information is not necessarily enough.

Research is out there which suggests that there may well be an argument for challenging the strongly neo-classical perspective that has defined the thinking about the returns associated with high performance.[20]

THE LAKE WOBEGON EFFECT

The story of the talent myth and its role in driving executive remuneration is another example of the 'Lake Wobegon Effect'. This, psychologists tell us, is the human tendency to rate one's capabilities and performance highly in relation to others. The term is derived from Lake Wobegon, created by the American author Garrison Keillor, a town where 'all the women are strong, all the men are good-looking, and all the children are above average'. Researchers Rachel M. Hayes and Scott Schaefer[21] in an article written in December 2008 looked into CEO pay as an example of this effect, having seen it being referenced increasingly by remuneration critics in the US:

No firm wants to admit to having a CEO who is below average, and so each firm wants its CEO's pay package to put him at or above the median pay level for comparable firms. It is well known that firms commonly disclose an intention to pay well; Bizjak et al. (2008) report that 73 out of 100 randomly selected firms 'mention targeting at least one component of pay at or above the peer group median or mean'. Of course, not every CEO can be paid more than average, and so (it is claimed) we see ever-increasing levels of CEO pay. The reasoning behind this effect was perhaps best summarized by former DuPont CEO Edward S. Woolard, Jr, speaking at a 2002 Harvard Business School roundtable on CEO pay (Elson, 2003): 'The main reason compensation increases every year is that most boards want their CEO to be in the top half of the CEO peer group, because they think it makes the company look strong. So when Tom, Dick, and Harry receive compensation increases in 2002, I get one too, even if I had a bad year ... [This leads to an] upward spiral.

The conclusions produced by their model suggest that a significant increase to a CEO's package or the introduction of a much more highly rewarded CEO than before could influence share price positively, suggesting performance to come and building in a more positive market view of performance. As Edward Woolard suggests above, once one goes there, well, everyone has to follow.

Public policy intervention can address this through, for example, changes to income tax treatment of earnings over a certain multiple or share option schemes or the like. However, ultimately change that makes a difference can only come if business leaders themselves act as stewards in the interests of all stakeholders in the firm and not as individuals acting in their own interest. The only people who can curb the excess for good are those who benefit from it. That is the real test of leadership: it will be interesting to see who really steps up and braves the cold shower for the greater good.

Chapter Eight
Less is More
The Future of Leadership and its Development in Organizations

The model of leaders as a super-race set apart and easy to tell apart from the rest of the herd is the leadership proposition of the L'Oreal generation. Whilst organizations need leadership, be they countries, businesses, churches or charities, what they don't need are self-obsessed leaders. Organizations are social structures, through which activities are distributed and managed. The process of deciding on what activities are undertaken, how they will be distributed and managed and how the organization will track progress is essentially one based on making relationships work. Effective relationships are consensual, collaborative and are based on a shared purpose. Much of what has gone before in this book comes together to reinforce the overriding importance of understanding human behaviour in the leadership of an organization. It requires an appreciation of the need to manage yourself in a structure where many relationships exist at the same time. In the best-led organizations leadership recognizes the importance of a collective commitment to a common ideology or purpose supported by a diversity of skills and talents. The value they create comes from the alignment of people to purpose and the debate and conflict that diverse perspectives bring to the delivery of that common goal.

A successful organization is one that delivers its core purpose to the satisfaction of its stakeholders. In a commercial organization satisfaction is measured in terms of the return achieved by the owners for their capital employed, in terms of job satisfaction and personal development by those who work within it, in terms of satisfaction with the product or service provided by its customers and in terms of the benefits, financial and other, brought to the communities within which it operates by civil society.

To do this well is a collective effort. Leaders play an important role: they give a shape to the common purpose of the organization, they coordinate the process of setting a vision of success and a direction of travel. They set the cultural tone and the values, they establish the standards by which performance will be managed. They engage stakeholders to build support for vision, direction and standards and they communicate constantly to reinforce all of the above and keep the organization aligned so that it works to deliver common goals. To do this well in anything other than a very small business requires a leadership team, not just one person. They have to work together to agree on these points; no leader can impose all this on an organization and expect it to stick. Leaders can drive, can be impatient, can push, but no leader can move faster than the slowest part of their organization. They either need to slow down, or fix it and to fix it requires other people to buy into the problem and then work to solve it.

Organizations fail when they build a culture and where an individual or small group of individuals dominate in such a way that they become what Henry Mintzberg[1] has described as 'leadership apart'. These leaders are unconnected from and insulated against conflict, challenge and debate. The culture is one of conformity and compliance with the views from the top. They are indeed the super-race. It is a proposition that Mintzberg argues, with some justification, has been promoted by many of the world's top business schools, and is at the heart of the talent myth first posited by McKinsey & Co nearly twenty years ago. This proposition is, as we have seen, fundamentally flawed. Yet despite this it has quickly gained ground, often through reinforcing the prejudices of those already at the top that they were there because they're worth it. The methods adopted in identifying and then developing 'top talent' have also been part of the problem. In Chapter Six I discussed the way in which the theory has also been driven by the Human Resources function, looking for a 'strategic' role in businesses and believing that with 'talent' it could find its way right onto the top table. Once in HR, with its reputation for establishing processes and systems that institutionalize whatever latest fad they are promoting, an associated industry of leader assessment and development and leader benchmarking has sprung up. This industry has become populated by specialist divisions of head-hunters, boutique psychometric assessment specialists, leadership development consultants and even business school academics. Regardless of the source of the expertise, businesses brought in these new advisors and through partnership with HR functions drove complex and costly individual assessment processes across the senior management population. These were normally described as 'talent reviews' and often had board level support and approval. They were positioned using phrases like 'assessing our talent bench strength' or some other such jargon which gave import and a hard business edge to what at best can be described as a questionable application of the principles of psychology.

These processes normally have four outcomes. First, they confirm the CEO and key board colleagues as entirely the right people to be in the roles they are. Secondly, they identify a group of people who they say have the potential to reach the very top, some of whom are always a surprise. Thirdly, they identify a group of often talented and able leaders as not having the potential for further promotion. Finally, they identify some whose leadership impact is such that they need to be moved on yet cannot be moved from the job they are in, and so are defined as organization 'blockers' and need to be dealt with. This latter group is then 'managed' by HR such that replacements with 'higher potential' – as defined and assessed by the specialist firm brought in to support the board in their 'talent review' – are found to replace them (sometimes from outside sourced through another division of the same firm). They then lose their jobs at a significant cost to the business because they fail to meet 'the standard' required to be a successful leader.

This leadership standard itself is worthy of some reflection. It is normally defined through some pseudo-scientific analysis of successful performers in senior roles already in place (with no regard to the quality of their teams or the economic context they are in) or an assessment against a 'benchmark' established through a similar analysis of 'successful performers' in other businesses. No one really questions the assessment methodology which is normally supported through reference to occupational psychology literature that few if any practitioners understand. In the manner of the Emperor's tailors, the advisors' word is taken with little or any critical assessment.

This is not only bad for organizations but also for those appointed into leadership roles. In a world obsessed with the cult of individuality, the cult of the leader is the acme of individualistic achievement and those who achieve it live the lives of modern gods. Once labelled a god, however, there is only one way to go: and it isn't up. The cult of individuality is an unforgiving religion. Once personalized, everything is your responsibility: all the success and all the failure. There is no collective sanctuary. There is no team, there is no sharing of accountability and there is no forgiveness if found wanting. Work done in the US suggests an increasing level of CEO turnover and a consequent reduction in CEO tenure in large corporations to around six years.[2] In the UK the more recent reports suggest this is around five years for both the FTSE 100 and the FTSE 250.[3]

The dominant leadership theories over the last thirty or so years have all been focused on the contribution of the individual leader. The leader was the prime differentiator of organizational success. They start with the proposition that if an organization can find the right set of characteristics in a person and these are developed fully over time then they will achieve their goals. The holy grail in all these propositions is a pool of 'top talent' all capable of taking the top job and driving the organization forward.

These theories are developed through the assessment of effective leaders in charge of organizations today. They exist on a continuum from the popular smiling faces of celebrities in the airport bookshop to the dense 11 point print of the academic journal consigned to the boxes at the back of the business school library. Those based on the hagiography of top CEOs and entrepreneurs follow the model of presenting broad themes that are taken from the life story that then develops into lessons that can be adopted by those wishing to be the next 'great one', delivered in the style of 'do this and don't do that' and you will succeed. Those emanating from the empiricist tradition take complex social science research techniques and use them to assess currently viewed 'high performers' in the hope of producing blueprints for developing success. Both make assumptions in their approach: that the organization will remain constant in its size, structure and complexity and that the economic, social and political environment will not change significantly. This is the problem with any behavioural model: it is practically impossible to build in anything other than a constant state in these regards but it is a significant flaw.

As any historian will tell you, there is a great deal of truth in the aphorism 'cometh the hour, cometh the man'. Few models of predictive behaviour based on what made the established leadership of their time successful would have identified Sir Winston Churchill, Nelson Mandela, Florence Nightingale or Konrad Adenauer as potential leaders of the future, yet circumstances gave them the chance to show that they were able to play a significant leadership role. The common links between these individuals would not be found in a list of leadership competencies. They are as diverse a grouping as one might find anywhere. What ties them together as effective leaders is their focus on the wider task, the greater good and the longer term. Their motivations were not financial, nor were they necessarily looking for status or high office. What is consistent about them is that at the core of their leadership approach was not just a personal vision but one that engaged many others. They also had the ability to pick people to work with who were as able, if not more so, than themselves. They worked with the team and in the team and for the team.

This is not an argument against individualism, quite the opposite, but it is an argument against celebrity in the management and leadership of organizations and the focus on a single individual. Outside of sports such as tennis and golf and areas such as the visual arts it is difficult if not impossible to argue that the individual's talents, attitude and drive are the defining sources of success or failure. Even here, the choice of coach, caddy or muse can influence whether or not the individual can achieve their full potential.

Since the late 1990s popular books on leadership have started to focus on a recognition of leadership as a collective or collaborative effort. Heenan and Bennis'[4] study of partnership in leadership of organizations produced a well argued proposition that there was an equally important role for a co-leader in modern organizations. It took examples from Berkshire Hathaway, Microsoft, Intel and Chrysler, in business, looked at great historical figures such as Chou En-lai and George C. Marshall and delved into fiction with an appreciation of Dr Watson's role in the success of Sherlock Holmes. This is, however, still a version of the 'heroic leader' model. The proposition is really about power-sharing between the already powerful and a paean to partnership rather than to a genuine collaborative effort across the whole organization. In the end the organization recipe is for a CEO and a COO, but no more than that. The co-leader is the modern day equivalent of the 'eminence grise': less instantly recalled than Louis XIV but equally as powerful as Cardinal Richelieu. What the book did do was address the issue of building a culture where the model of a single all-powerful leader was not the defining characteristic which starts with the proposition that we should 'celebrate the enterprise not celebrity'.[5]

Within their range of organization solutions that would help achieve this goal are two things that should contribute to a recasting of the thinking about developing effective leadership: first, the need to institutionalize dissent and secondly to set team goals, not individual ones.

More recently, Goffee and Jones[6] incorporated the importance of the notion of 'followership' and looked at what it took for people to accept and engage with a leader in organizations. This has had a significant impact in leadership thinking, but surprisingly less so in organizational practice. There are three key points. The first counters the orthodoxy in leadership development that began with 'Action Centred Leadership'[7] and argues that leadership is situational. Certain leadership styles and approaches, they argue, will not work in certain situations. This is not 'situational leadership'[8] which is the theory that leaders must change style and approach to suit the circumstances: it argues that people have to be changed when the situation demands. They believe that leadership is also non-hierarchical. They argue that leadership is required and occurs throughout an organization rather than just at the top. Organizations succeed, they suggest, where leadership is demonstrated by people in their roles: if you like this is an extension of the engagement work discussed in Chapter Six. An engaged employee is far more likely to take the lead and act for the greater good. Their final key point is that leadership is relational, i.e. that it requires people to respond willingly by following the lead set and that this will only happen if they feel they can engage with the leader at a personal level.

The focus of the book was on the individual leader and what he or she could do to ensure they developed the skills to adjust to the situation and to create willing followers. Its central proposition was that those who get followed are those who are best at knowing themselves and are able to show themselves to others so that they are seen as authentic. The proposition most often referred to from the book is that an effective leader knows how to be themselves with skill. Whilst this is a positive proposition as far as it goes, it is however still an extension of the paradigm of the heroic leader, rather than an organization prescription that builds an authentic business.

Indeed one might well argue that Goffee and Jones have lighted upon a universal requirement for working successfully in any collaborative undertaking regardless of the role undertaken. If everyone thought about being themselves with skill then we would have the basis for successful collaboration. Anyone with any experience of leading in organizations will tell you that it is the lack of collaboration across organizational boundaries that is most often one of the largest barriers to success. To do this we need less focus on leaders and more on what sort of leadership it takes to drive a successful outcome through a collective structure. The challenge for leadership development in organizations is, therefore, more than introducing any individually focused solution, but rather finding a structure and an approach that transforms leadership from being leader-centric to being outcome-centric.

This is a cultural question, not one of choosing the right training and development. Organization cultures are complex things but they can be defined simply as 'the way we do things around here'. There are far more complex and academic versions out there, the most famous being that of Edgar Schein who described it as:

> A pattern of basic assumptions, invented, discovered, or developed by a given group, as it learns to cope with its problems of external adaptation and internal integration, that has worked well enough to be considered valid and, therefore is to be taught to new members as the correct way to perceive, think, and feel in relation to those problems.[9]

I prefer my definition, though, not just because it is shorter and therefore more memorable, but because in my view culture is not a theoretical construct, but a daily reality for all of us. Whether in our paid employment, in the voluntary organizations we support, or in our communities, we face the challenge of understanding and adjusting to the prevailing culture. This culture comes about because each of these organizations has some values that are shared so widely that they drive an accepted set of beliefs which in turn define what is the generally accepted way of acting in any set of circumstances. In other words, remember when you first joined your current organization and you spent the inevitable first few weeks asking how you got things done? If you think back on it you may well recall that the most often repeated answer you got was likely to have been words that said in one way or another: 'Well, the way we do [whatever] here is …'

One of the reasons it is so difficult to change processes, systems and behaviours in organizations is precisely this: you are in effect attempting to change tens of thousands of conversations that take place every day. For a new way of doing things, of behaving, of measuring effective performance, every conversation has to be adjusted, which requires everyone to accept the change, emotionally as well as intellectually, such that they make a conscious effort to answer the 'how to' question differently.[10]

So how do we develop organizations and the leadership culture within them to build a more authentic business? According to the latest HR bestseller by Dave Ulrich and his collaborator Norm Smallwood, *Leadership Brand*, by approaching leadership in the same way as you would a core product or service.[11] Now Ulrich and Smallwood have been the victims of HR zeal in the past when their carefully argued HR model was wrongly interpreted as an organizational as opposed to an intellectual solution for thinking through how HR could and should add value to an organization. Their original 'HR Model' proposed a way through which HR could think strategically about what added most value and where to allocate time and resources. It rapidly transmogrified into an organizational orthodoxy in which HR, desperate to be seen as 'strategic', ditched the less value-adding of what they did in one of two ways: into a service centre or into the lap of the line manager. Needless to say with service centres being about as successful as your bank or utility supplier's call centre neither line managers nor staff was too pleased. It was the adoption of what is now known as the 'Ulrich' model that created the HR business partner, ready and willing of course to work with you on your 'war for talent'.

So Ulrich and Smallwood, taking a similar approach, have moved into leadership and their book offers some real insights into the problems associated with fashionable HR approaches. Their list includes competency models of leadership development which deliver generic rather than specific outcomes, eye-catching training activities which are unaligned with and unconnected to the strategy of the organization and expensive culture programmes with no ownership from the top. These they argue undercut rather than reinforce the laudable goals that the organization was trying to achieve. This they argue is because much of what is done internally is focused only on the internal. They point out that unless the external experience of customers and other key stakeholders aligns with the internally driven leadership imperatives then there is less chance of long-term success. They rightly argue that the organization has to ensure consistency of the experience right the way from raw materials input through to customer experience of the final product. These are all good points that should be taken seriously by anyone wanting to move leadership development forward in their organization.

The problem with the 'leadership is a brand' approach is in the insistence of linking an insightful analysis of leadership impact with the far less convincing proposition that somehow this can be branded and indeed, even more worryingly, linked to 'personal' brands. In the end, having argued that leadership is more important than celebrity leaders, Ulrich and Smallwood finish on why this is good for your own branding and the importance of personal brands being congruent with the firm's leadership brand. This results in tying it back to the very essence of what underpins celebrity itself through encouraging leaders to develop a 'personal leadership brand statement'. They provide a process for so doing including completing a part written sentence allowing you to choose the 'six words that best reflect what you want to be known for'. Rather than describing themselves, warts and all, leaders are encouraged to describe an aspirational self which can then be developed, pack-aged and communicated in the manner of a brand.

We are not brands, we are human beings. If we accept that we can be 'marketed' then we accept that there is value in being a perfect proposition that meets the needs of all stakeholders at all times. We buy the fact that we are no different from L'Oreal's cosmetic products, we work without blemish and have a positive outcome every time. This is the antithesis of authenticity and also a denial of our own humanity. It is critical to separate our branded product or service from ourselves. We need to know our contribution to it, the way we can add greatest value to it and the risks associated with failing to engage all those in the organization with its delivery to our customers. We are not, however senior we are, the be all and end all of it. Defining the relationship that is leadership as a brand diminishes it to the level of a strategic lever. Leadership is the understanding of your own values and their importance in all that you do and being prepared to act on them. Even if that means leaving the organization that you are in today because it refuses to act in the way you and others know it should.

As Hegel asserted over 200 years ago, we all understand the difference between right and wrong and if we can't end the wrong, and it transgresses a core value, then the choice is clear: support a lie or leave. This is, of course, a very difficult decision and is made even more so when the systems and structures of an organization reinforce what any rational analysis from outside it would suggest is mistaken and misguided behaviour that destroys value and/or reputation. This, for example, was clearly the circumstance that brought so much approbation down on the UK's House of Commons when the details of their allowances were exposed in a national newspaper. Whilst the application of the system by the majority of MPs was entirely within the rules that applied, the rules that applied were so egregious and so entirely without any comprehension of the likely reaction of electors, that very few of the 656 members escaped without some form of criticism. It was also the circumstance that undermined the leaders of AIG and others in the US after their bonus mechanisms were revealed in the aftermath of the financial crisis.

These circumstances arise in business when owners do not have transparency and the leverage to act when they see things they know are not in the best interests of the organization as a whole. Part of the changes we need to make in 21st century organizations is to restore the connection with the real owners of businesses as opposed to those few fund managers who act as their proxies. In this we need to challenge the leadership role of the board and demand a greater sense of ownership from our well connected and well remunerated non-executive directors.

CHANGING APPROACHES TO LEADERSHIP

In this manifesto for a more authentic business it is these changes that will give organizations the greatest challenge, not because they are any more difficult than those associated with talent or remuneration, but because they will impact everyone if they are to be successful. They require a significant redefinition of roles and responsibilities, particularly at the top. Regardless of the difficulty, without them business will never completely re-build its reputation for efficient and effective use of resources to create wealth from which everyone will benefit.

BUILD A LEADERSHIP EXPECTATION FOR THE BOARD

Remarkably for the body that sits at the apex of an organization hierarchy, there is little acceptance of a leadership role for the board. They have accepted roles in governance, risk management, corporate responsibility and strategic financial resource allocation and financial reporting but leadership is abdicated to the executive committee. This division of responsibilities between those who represent the interests of the owners of a business and the stewards whom the owners have entrusted with maximizing the returns from their capital employed in the enterprise sits at the heart of what is wrong in modern corporations. No self-respecting entrepreneur would leave the shaping and expression of the corporate core purpose, the setting of values, management culture and strategic performance standards to others. They understand the role that these activities play in ensuring they get the best possible returns from their business. Yet non-executive directors in many major corporations, elected by owners to act as their representatives, do not own these areas for themselves. They may get them presented at the end of a long internal process, they may be asked to sign them off but by the time they reach the board they are more often than not a done deal.

This is a reflection of the drive in North America and in the EU to separate the executive day-to-day running of the organization from the strategic direction of the business and to provide a degree of supervisory overview of the activities of the CEO and other senior officers. As boards have become increasingly dominated by the 'non-executives' so they have become increasingly distanced from the organizations that they supervise. This leads to a number of risks, the most significant being that the non-executives fail to get into the business and understand what it is they are taking responsibility for. This was clearly the case in a number of the spectacular corporate collapses of recent years and was a particular feature of the financial crisis of 2008/9 where it emerged that many banks had directors with little or no understanding of the sector and little or no insight into the products and processes that were underpinning financial performance. Others will include the inability to judge the appropriateness or otherwise of adopted values, performance reward structures and proposed criteria for appointment of senior executives.

If the executive is to be supervised effectively then boards have to engage fully. This inevitably means that non-executive directors should be limited to the number of such directorships they hold. Just as importantly we should set clear expectations for them as leaders. Up till now leadership in business has been seen as the CEO and his or her direct reports. But what about the Chairman? Shouldn't they be seen as a leader and just as importantly held accountable for the leadership of the business? Non-executive leadership is an incredible skill. It is probably best exemplified by the role of constitutional monarch or a president in a system of parliamentary government. Chairmen need training and development to be effective in these roles just as much as CEOs do in theirs.

If boards are to represent owners' interests then, whilst not necessarily being required to work full time, they must take back responsibility for leading the organization. Board agendas need to move from obsession with the process of risk management to the active management of key areas of risk. These include the setting of values and the running of programmes to build compliance, effective communication of the long-term goals and interests of owners to everyone in the organization, role modelling the attitudes and behaviour owners expect to see throughout their business and holding the senior executives to account for the day-to-day decisions that they take.

BE EXPLICIT ABOUT VALUES AND WHAT HAPPENS WHEN THEY ARE IGNORED

All organizations have values: they are what define the way they behave towards customers, suppliers, their employees and wider civil society. What has always intrigued me is that they are not always the values they espouse on their websites and in their annual reports. Indeed research conducted by several sources[12] shows that the values espoused by global corporations are remarkably similar, yet we experience them very differently. Enron's values[13] of Respect, Integrity, Communication and Excellence were on the surface the sorts of values that would reflect the model of business that I am arguing for in this book: in fact most of the analyses of Enron's demise have concluded that its real values were 'performance at any cost' which is what drove all the behaviour from CEO Kenneth Lay down. Enron leaders behaved congruently with the real values. What owners and potential owners and many adoring business school academics failed to spot was the real value set that drove the business: they bought the leadership brand, not the leadership reality.

Rosabeth Moss Kanter[14] has argued that there is a strong potential synergy between financial performance and attention to community and social needs. In a book focused on reforming the North American model of management she asserts that there is a unique competitive advantage from reflecting the values and expectations of the up and coming generation of professionals, and growth opportunities from stressing corporate values and restraining executive egos when building alliances and merging acquisitions. She highlights the following advantages for placing explicit values at the heart of a business proposition:

Competitive differentiation: An emphasis on corporate values builds specific lines of business and strengthens an organization's brand.

Public accountability via end-to-end responsibility: Corporate values help meet the public's request that organizations should know, care, and communicate about all aspects of their products and services.

Rationale for long-term thinking: Corporate values that include operating philosophies or principles of sustainability help organizations create continuity. Such values help them avoid 'short-termism'.

Common vocabulary and guidance for consistent decisions: Corporate values are an essential guide to organizations that need to make fast decisions and take quick action in far-flung or differentiated operations.

Talent magnets and motivation machines: People are mobile but just as importantly, as we have seen from work on commitment and engagement, they are attracted to organizations whose corporate values match their key concepts and ideals. People stay with organizations they are proud to be associated with.

'Human' control systems – peer review and a self-control system: Belief in corporate values strengthens peer responsibility for keeping one another aligned; it also generates self-guidance and self-policing. Such human control systems do not work perfectly but they reduce the need for rules and free people up to act autonomously.

Values come not from a single leader nor from all leaders but from a common commitment and belief system held by a community of people who have joined the organization voluntarily. They are not part of a brand or PR proposition: they are about what holds us together and why we are here. They should be different in some respects to reflect different sectors and different economic situations. It is OK to have a value that says we do not offer jobs for life, but whilst you are here we'll respect you, challenge you and develop you. No-one says this right now but there are plenty of good corporations out there who live by this, and whose employees accept it as perfectly reasonable. Authentic businesses have authentic values and can show you, transparently, that they behave by them and are happy to be judged by them.

Finally on values, reward and recognition in the organization have to reflect the importance of sticking to the declared values. It must be clear to all stakeholders that those who reflect the values succeed and are rewarded and those who do not are, if the breach is serious enough, actively removed from employment. An increasing number of organizations now do this through having a clearly communicated 'Code of Conduct' which lays out acceptable and unacceptable actions, protects whistleblowers from raising concerns about actions taken by senior executives and lays down the potential consequences for a breach of the code. If you put one of these in you have to be prepared to dismiss anyone found to be in serious breach. This does not mean coming to a negotiated settlement and funding payments in lieu of notice and tying it all up in a legal agreement that binds both parties to silence. It means a dismissal for gross misconduct and we'll see each other in court.

REINFORCE COLLECTIVE ACCOUNTABILITY THROUGH PERFORMANCE MANAGEMENT PROCESSES

Team goals, team accountability and team rewards are powerful ways of removing the cult of individuality from the organization. As I have discussed previously there are ways of differentiating between individual contributions that are entirely consistent with a collaborative as opposed to an internally competitive approach. If the organization has a clear purpose and a clear strategic direction then a few simple big objectives can be used as headlines for every person showing their contribution to the overall goals and how they link in and have to work with others to achieve them.

Just as importantly in this is ensuring that the organization has institutionalized dissent. This isn't about putting those who are deliberately oppositionist on the top team, but it is about ensuring that there are plenty of opportunities for those with concerns, doubts or insights they believe leaders need to have before they make decisions to input into the decision-making process. 'My door is always open' is not one of these opportunities. Active engagement through informal conversations, formal meetings, suggestion schemes, open email boxes, etc. are all signs that encourage people to contribute. Welcome all contributions, take seriously those that are constructive, note those that are not and ask for solutions as well as criticisms. Respond positively if they come through again in a more constructive way. Build close trusting relationships with one or two people right at the bottom of the organization who are unafraid of answering straight questions and who, as they build trust in you, will offer unsolicited views and opinions that could give you real insight. Make sure your customers and suppliers are as engaged in this process as your employees.

STOP DEVELOPING LEADERS AND START DEVELOPING ORGANIZATIONAL LEADERSHIP

This is going to sound as though I am about to undermine my role as a Professor of Leadership in a major European business school – and my past tenure as Dean of another – but I don't believe that there is any merit in development programmes that are based on building heroic leaders as individuals. All they do is reinforce the exclusivity of the individual being developed, the importance of them as an individual and their position as a member of your very own super-human species. I have held roles in development in both business and in business education. The most effective leadership programmes I have been associated with were those that were focused on developing a consistent and commonly understood leadership approach across the organization. This approach is based on shared values and widely applied business processes. They created a common language, set common expectations, enabled the communication and discussion of common messages and reinforced the importance of diversity of style and personal approaches. They built a collective not an individual expectation. They were about the organization, not the individual.

The secret of these programmes is that, without exception, they were linked to a major strategic objective that was associated with a corporate goal. In Cadbury Schweppes we ran three programmes that started with the board and went right through the organization reinforcing the same messages and asking for the same behavioural response. The first introduced the understanding and business application of economic value and economic cost to resource allocation and strategy development. It was about thinking through shareowner value, about creating value rather than destroying it and the changes in behaviour that would have to happen at every level if we were to make better decisions and deliver better returns. It helped deliver a doubling of the share price in a four-year period. The second took leadership teams and got them to work together in highly innovative ways to help them support new ideas and products. It introduced a radically different approach to performance coaching which was based on 'The Inner Game'[15] which was adopted by many of our operating companies as the standard approach for people management. Lastly, there were programmes that changed the standards and processes around global brand management, which for the first time established a common way of doing marketing across every single brand and operating company. Each of these introduced new ways of doing things and new demands on leadership across the organization. They made it a collective responsibility, they reinforced and role modelled the behaviours that supported the values of the organization. They had measurable business outcomes to which they were linked, thereby improving the chances of a sustainable change back in the business once the programme was over.

INVEST IN INDIVIDUAL PERSONAL EFFECTIVENESS

The individual programmes that do work best are those associated with improving individual personal effectiveness. Many of these in Europe and North America have been wrongly re-branded as leadership programmes. This is more a reflection of what sells well to individuals and their companies than because they specifically reflect on the nature of leadership. At their best they help people address the question: 'Why should anyone work with you?' They build an understanding of effective team working, personal communication and interaction and the importance of personal development time with a mentor, coach or other supportive individual.

For many new managers as well as those in more senior leadership roles, early investment in the range of personal skills and techniques that improve the effectiveness of their organizational behaviour can transform results. This is where external programmes come into their own. The freedom to test and experiment with new approaches in a risk-free environment where there is little if any chance of reports getting back to colleagues and bosses can really help people open up to change and to make changes to how they do things. This is not an advert for training programmes, far from it. Coaching, mentoring, informal discussion and problem solving sessions at work all have their place and need to be seen as part of the organization's commitment to people at every level.

WHY LESS IS MORE

Leadership is one of the great examples in modern organization development where less is more. The heroic leader is a failed god and any organization still running processes, systems and programmes that are based on the assumption that this is what they need should throw in the towel now and stop wasting scarce resources.

Organizations need leadership defined as a transparent adherence to a clear set of core values through which everyone in the organization will be judged by the owners of the business, their customers and wider society. To achieve this, organizations should be investing in programmes, systems and processes that support their values and ensure that their values are distinctive where they should and could be. They should look to run themselves as collaborative enterprises where leadership roles are about coordinating, engaging and aligning as much as they are about taking difficult decisions and making unpopular change stick.

Leadership development is a whole-organization concern. It needs to be owned and led by the board whose role is to insist on a clear purpose, strong core values and a programme that ensures these are driven through the organization and that strategies and performance standards and reward programmes enhance the purpose and mirror the values. Boards have to have an active leadership role just as much as a CEO and their fellow executives. In a collaborative undertaking leadership is a shared, not an exclusive responsibility.

The future for leadership development in organizations is to concern itself less with the leader and to focus more on the building of the appropriate values, culture and aligned management systems and processes at every level of the corporation. There is a role for the wealth-creating sector in acting as a leader in its own right influencing public policy and the attitudes of civil society to create positive and supportive conditions for wealth creators in the interests of all. Whilst the leaders in major corporations continue to defend their pay and benefits, continue to turn a blind eye to behaviour that does not live up to their espoused public value systems and continue to pack their boards with non-executives who do not align with the owners' interests then we, the general public will continue to regard them with distrust. Today's wealth creators will have to change their attitude to leadership significantly if the rest of us are to accept that they have any right to lead either in their own organizations or more widely.

Conclusion
The Importance of Being Earnest
The Price of the Cult and the Value
of Leadership

It was Oscar Wilde who defined a cynic as 'a man who knows the price of everything and the value of nothing.'[1] More recently it was Raj Patel who used this phrase to propound a thesis that the price mechanism of the market had blinded us to seeing the real value in our world and what it and its fundamentalist 'free market' proponents were doing that was destroying it. What we need today, he argued, is to dismantle much of what the market has constructed that is destroying humanity. His long list includes consumerism, private ownership of strategic industries and banking. He argues that the power of money is so toxic that the only way to take on the market is through direct action and the imposition of an activist model of democracy. His anger is palpable, his desire is to restore a sense of real value to the world we live in. His goal is to deliver environmental and economic sustainability for all the world's people. His proposition is summed up in this line:

> A sustainable future will need markets, but ones that are kept firmly in their place lest the motives, passions and resources that a few people are able to derive from them continue to corrupt the rest of society and the planet.[2]

This proposition, that we are all victims of market fundamentalism, is as fallacious now as it was in its earlier guise in the writings of Marx or the later socialists who followed him. There are victims of the masked Zapatistas in Mexico whom he celebrates as the perfect democrats just as much as there are victims of fraudulent behaviour in the market economy. But the argument that the market is somehow morally more culpable is one that is given succour and credibility by the behaviour of many of those who have reached the top of the most significant and public representations of the market in action: global corporations. The ideas expounded by Patel, Naomi Klein and others are making inroads in politics in particular and in civil society in general by using the excesses, the mistakes and the unethical behaviour that have been exposed by the history of corporate collapse, ineffective and complacent regulation and the global financial crisis to create a sense of conspiracy against the needs and interests of ordinary people.

The opponents of the market portray today's global corporations as out of control, out of contact with the values and concerns of the communities within which they operate and out to trash the planet. The list they use to justify their position on global capitalism is familiar to us all, from the dishonesty exposed in the collapses of Enron, WorldCom, Tyco and Parmalat, through the executive complaisance with poor corporate governance in Hollinger and RBS and the failure of risk and activity management in BP, Goldman Sachs and Northern Rock to the accusations of promotion of 'poor' product and its impact on health and well-being aimed at MacDonalds, Nestlé, Kraft and others in 'big food'.

Whilst in the specific incidents with which we are all familiar we would accept many of the criticisms aimed at corporations, the extraction of a general point that claims deliberate and wanton damage in the interests of a few wealthy shareowners is way off the mark. What we are seeing, particularly with the rise of the global corporation being mirrored by a rise in global communication, is an increasing focus on and awareness of corporations of all sizes and their importance to modern society. Much greater levels of scrutiny exist today than did forty years ago. As a consequence, many more mistakes, errors of judgement and deliberate acts of dishonesty are being revealed. Does this reflect a greater incidence of dishonesty? It is difficult to say and certainly there is no research at this stage which indicates any sense of a relative increase in such incidents compared to twenty to thirty years ago.

What we can say with some degree of confidence is that today business generally faces greater scrutiny. This comes at a time when it has combined with greater demands from a different mix of owners for capital growth as well as regular income. Given that capital growth is something that is driven as much by sentiment and market activity unrelated to the business as much as it is by directly influenced activity we can see the pressures on business leadership have mounted considerably over the past thirty to forty years. Business now faces a substantial regulatory regime that has promoted the importance of risk management processes. These have been driven down through organizations in such a way that the existence of a paper trail to prove that risks have been reviewed and assessed is more important to the corporation than a risk management mindset which thought strategically about risk and then acted to reduce it. This combination of pressures can drive one of two responses: a legalistic one or an open and empowering one. Regrettably, for most large corporations, it is the former that has triumphed over the latter in the mistaken belief that this was more likely to protect the interests of the owner, when really all this does is act in the interests of the steward.

Transparency in business drives power in two directions: externally to owners and customers and other major stakeholders such as regulators and downwards to staff on the ground who feel able to act in the best long-term interests of the organization without fear of reprisal or criticism. Had BP's senior management empowered their ground team in the Gulf of Florida they may well have avoided the 2010 disaster that befell their owners. After all, we now know the team on the ground apparently felt what they were doing was too risky to continue. No doubt the enquiry that will inevitably follow will judge how true this assertion will turn out to be, however, this on top of all that has gone before, has to mark a turning point in corporate management and leadership.

The cult of the celebrity leader demands a successful, above average, incumbent. The modern global corporation has, at the encouragement of their stewards, provided all the levers to ensure their leader is a superior performer regardless of reality. The talent myth provides the intellectual justification for their acceptance as above average. The reward structures provide the incentive to be above average and the legalistic response to operating in the 21st century provides the processes and the mechanics to continue to report and promote themselves as above average performers with far less scrutiny by (and accountability to) the real owners of the business.

In an article in the UK daily *The Independent*[3] David Prosser points out that it is unsurprising in these circumstances that it is impossible to spend more than five minutes talking to a CEO before they begin to use words like transformation and historic. He argues that the weight of expectation of delivering a dynamic dream of the future is one reason why CEOs are obsessed with takeovers, despite the weight of evidence that they are rarely successful. When, like Tidjane Thiam, CEO of the UK insurance giant Prudential, their transformational gambit fails, a CEO once lionized for being the first black person in a FTSE 100 leadership role was reduced to negotiating unsuccessfully with shareowners for his job. Prosser, quoting a UK leadership expert, is pointing out that successful CEOs often come from tough backgrounds, have suffered childhood adversities and sustain long-lasting family support, even if family life is non-existent. It is what makes them successful. Prosser asks is this really the template we want for our leaders:

> Should the chief executive office be filled only by people toughened up during a childhood brush with adversity, and only then if they are prepared to sacrifice their personal relationships for the sake of the job? No wonder so many chief executives, successful or otherwise, lose touch with reality.

This is where we are today: a wealth-creating sector whose ability to generate sustainable sources of wealth is critical to us meeting the challenges of 21st century; yet whose credibility and acceptability to wider society as a legitimate partner in this enterprise is at its lowest levels ever. This is the legacy of the L'Oreal generation.

It need not be like this. Strong confident leadership from business to put right what is wrong with its current approach to leaders and leadership would create a more authentic business. I define an authentic business as one with the following characteristics:

- A clear purpose, obvious and transparent to owners, employees, suppliers and customers alike.
- One that sells products or services that are audited for adherence to the best global standards associated with employment, raw material sourcing and environmental impact.
- One that invests in the future of the enterprise and in the future of the communities within which it operates.
- One that rewards all its employees fairly and in proportion to their level of responsibility and personal contribution.
- One that pays its fair share of taxes rather than invests in elaborate schemes to minimize them.
- One that people want to work with and work for.
- One that is conscious of its obligations to its owners and ensures they get the best possible return for their investment.

This is a business which stakeholders from across civil society would engage with in a positive and supportive manner. Many businesses, especially small and medium-sized companies, are already run like this. This isn't just because of the fact that they don't have the resources that can be directed away from the business to the stewards without immediate and significant impact on the business. They believe in these principles. Having said this, much of business needs to clean up its act: or watch impotently from the sidelines whilst others, less sympathetic to the conditions for business success, probably influenced by the neo-socialist agenda, act on behalf of society as a whole.

The manifesto for change is clear. Leadership has to become organization-centric not leader-centric and to achieve this we have to reject the talent myth that has distorted so much of corporate practice in the recruitment, retention and development of people. It needs replacing with an inclusive and diverse mindset that looks for what everyone can do to deliver the corporate core purpose. It has to value everyone's contribution equally and it must reward it fairly.

Rewards at the top of the organization have to bear some relative relationship with those further down at a level that all in the organization accept as appropriate and with which the owners of the organization have to agree. I have argued for a maximum multiple of forty times the average earnings of those employed excluding the CEO and their direct reports and that this should cover the total cost of remuneration. There may well be arguments for a greater figure or a lesser one, but whatever the eventual outcome we need to have the debate and it needs owner approval. Owner agreement cannot be left to those who act as proxies for them. Remuneration principles and plans should be referred directly to all owners of the capital employed in the business however their interest is held. If they ask fund managers to act as proxies for them then they need to ensure that these fund managers cast their votes in accordance with their wishes, not in accordance with the needs of their own remuneration plans.

The board needs to reassert its traditional role as the leadership of the business, as opposed to the leadership of the executive organization that is employed by the business to deliver its core purpose. They should step in to own values and how they are built, reinforced and protected. Great values accepted and applied throughout an organization reduce significantly the chances of poor decision-making and cock-up. Board directors need to focus on one or two organizations, they need training and development and they have to have an understanding of the business sector or be engaged in an intensive programme of induction. The appointment of board members must be taken out of the control of the executive and out of closed appointments processes dominated by a few well networked head-hunters.

We have to dismantle the cult of the leader. This is one of the most difficult things of all to do as it is so closely linked to the wider social phenomenon of our obsession with celebrity. There are signs that the generation that is entering work today is looking for a very different kind of society than that created by the L'Oreal generation. They are far more concerned with the externalities than internal needs and drivers. For example, a recent report[4] for AIESEC, the international student organization on climate change, shows that 75% of young people from all parts of the world thought that organizations were not doing enough to address the impact of climate change. They see it as a political problem and they want actions taken now.

Andy Warhol is quoted in an exhibition catalogue from 1968 as saying that 'in the future everybody will be world famous for fifteen minutes.'[5] Today with hundreds of television channels, thousands of magazines and millions of online pages to fill with content we are nearer that reality than ever before. But whilst this may be the direction of popular culture it doesn't have to be the direction of business. To change we have to be prepared to junk the Lake Wobegon syndrome and accept that sometimes and in some things we are all below average. This is potentially the most liberating proposition in leadership that we could introduce into modern business. What it says is that 'Mary Poppins Managers' are as likely to exist as weapons of mass destruction in Iraq and spending time working with the imperfect is far more likely to deliver value than searching for leadership nirvana. We should take out of organizations competency models that persuade people that perfection is attainable and reinforce those that promote diversity. This would make it acceptable to have real, human, difficult-to-get-around faults. This isn't about rejecting feedback. We need processes that point faults out and coaching or development activities that may help ameliorate therm. There are many things that people asked to take on leadership roles in organizations can and should try and do well. But we should put them in these roles because first and foremost they have the humility to recognize that they are asking people to give up their right to lead for themselves. This is particularly true in circumstances where we face challenges of which we have no previous experience.

In today's world leadership success will come from being able to judge the techniques we choose to manage people through constant change where there is no clear outcome or certain success. Marty Linksy and Ronald Heifetz's[6] work on adaptive change at all levels in society outlines the problems of modern leadership succinctly. They draw us back, however, to another time where change was driving society into the unknown by reminding us of Machievelli's advice to his Prince that in change the best you'll get is half-hearted support. As a leader in a changing world far more is stacked against you than in the old and applying rules from a time where leaders were the authorities with all of the answers is one sure fire way to fail:

People cannot see at the beginning of the adaptive process that the new situation will be any better than the current condition. What they do see clearly is the potential for loss. People frequently avoid painful adjustments in their lives if they can postpone them, place the burden on someone else, or call someone to the rescue. When fears and passions run high, people can become desperate as they look to authorities for the answers. This dynamic renders adaptive contexts inherently dangerous.

Their argument is that when people look to authorities for easy answers at best they get short-term fixes at the expense of long-term solutions. They expect the leader to know what to do, and under that pressure of expectation, those in authority frequently end up disappointing people, or they get replaced in the belief that a new 'leader' will solve the problem they have failed to address. The bigger the change the greater resistance will be and the greater the danger to those who lead. For this reason, people in positions of authority understandably often try to avoid the dangers, either consciously or subconsciously, by transforming the challenge into a technical problem rather than one that requires a fundamental shift in mindset. This is the single most common form of leadership failure.

It is the biggest challenge facing those of us who want the market to succeed. We could respond to the challenges in this book by introducing more regulations, greater audit provisions, tighter bonus structures and the like. If we do, we won't create the change we need to ensure that the only wealth-creating process we know works has a chance of succeeding in the future.

Corporations will only exist successfully if they can put more people into leadership positions who understand the difference between right and wrong. People who have developed their understanding through experience, who have the relational skills to work effectively across many cultures and perspectives and who can see the wider global context within which they are operating and through which their reputation will be built or destroyed. To do this they have to begin a process of significant and systemic change.

This is not a message that some leaders in global corporations will be too happy to hear. Some of them have too much of their credibility tied up in the current way of doing things. Some will think first and foremost about the impact on their current way of life and some will ignore the evidence and continue to regurgitate the mantra of the 'war for talent'. For those willing to give this manifesto serious consideration I would ask them to think not of themselves but of their shareowners, the real ones that is, not the fund managers. These shareowners are also their customers and their suppliers and quite often their employees. They are also the voters, the community leaders and the members and supporters of NGOs. We, the shareowners, need you to change and if you do you'll find us your most supportive stakeholders. So when we look at you as voters, as pressure group supporters and as members of the community in which you operate we'll be far more likely to ensure that you get support in your objective to create the most wealth you can. That's the advantage of being an authentic business.

Notes

INTRODUCTION

1 Great Britain is the United Kingdom minus the province of Northern Ireland, so consists of England, Scotland and Wales.

2 Source: The Poverty Site (http://www.poverty.org.uk/09/index.shtml).

3 Dictionary.com, 'lifestyle,' in Dictionary.com Unabridged. Source location: Random House, Inc. http://dictionary.reference.com/browse/lifestyle. Available: http://dictionary.reference.com.

4 Sources: http://www.independent.co.uk/news/uk/politics/whos-who-on-the-new-guest-list-at-chequers-it-helps-if-you-are-highbrow-874855.html.

5 http://news.bbc.co.uk/1/hi/6506365.stm regarding Blair's holiday hosts.

6 Sourced from: http://www.achievemax.com/bookreviews.

7 St Peter's denial of Christ, St Paul's usury, St Mary Magdeline's profession are probably three of the best known examples that support the proposition that sainthood in the Christian tradition is not about perfection in life.

8 The core story of Buddha in finding no happiness in either fabulous wealth or abject poverty but in a middle path, that understands that it is not the experience of pleasure, but craving for that pleasure over and above anything else, that brings unhappiness is a dramatic contrast to the slavish materialism of the L'Oreal generation.

9   Management Today's Britain's Most Admired Companies awards are the UK's business Oscars. (Source: http://www.haymarket.com/management_today/multi/mtandrsquos_britainandrsquos_most_admired_companies_awards/default.aspx).

10 Source: http://www.guardian.co.uk/business/2009/feb/10/abn-amro-columnists-predictions.

11 Aristotle, *Politics*.

12 'Gallup International releases its 5th Annual Davos Survey' http://www.gallup.com.pk/Polls/18-1-08.pdf.

13 http://www.edelman.co.uk/files/trust-barometer-2009-summary.pdf.

CHAPTER ONE

1   Sir Michael Levey (1962, 1968), *From Giotto to Cezanne, A concise history of painting*.

2   *The Oxford Dictionary of Quotations* (1975) cites Dulaure's 'Histoire de Paris' as attributing this remark to Louis XIV.

3   For a concise summary of enlightened despotism see E. N. Williams (1980) *The Penguin Dictionary of English and European History*, Penguin, Harmondsworth, Middlesex.

4   The descriptor often used by the old landed aristocracy was 'nouveau riche' meaning one who has recently acquired (usually ostentatious) wealth. The French term was probably adopted to reinforce the educational deficit of these newly rich individuals who were unlikely to have learnt any foreign language or to possess the degree of refinement associated with things French of the period.

5   http://www.democraticaudit.com/download/Findings6LR.pdf.

6   The source of this is attributed to many people. Shakespeare's Hamlet instructing on dramatic art said: '... the purpose of playing, whose end, both at the first and now, was and is, to hold as 'twere the mirror up to nature: to show virtue her feature, scorn her own image, and the very age and body of the time his

form and pressure'. (Hamlet Act 3, scene 2, 17–24). This was famously disputed by Bertolt Brecht who argued that '[a]rt is not a mirror held up to reality, but a hammer with which to shape it'.

7   Malcolm Higgs, 'Leadership – the long line: A view on how we can make sense of leadership in the 21st century', Henley Working Paper series HWP 0207, 2002.

8   F. W. Taylor (1911) *The Principles of Scientific Management*, Harper & Brothers, New York and London.

9   Source: http://www.amazon.co.uk/leadership-Books/s/qid=1269 084065/ref=sr_pg_74?ie=UTF8&sort=-pubdate&keywords=lea dership&bbn=266239&rh=n%3A266239%2Cn%3A%21102 5612%2Ck%3Aleadership&page=74.

10   M. Belbin, (1981) *Management Teams*, London; Heinemann.

11   R. E. Boyatzis (1982) *The Competent Manager*, John Wiley & Sons Inc, New York, New York.

12   R. E. Boyatzis (1982) *The Competent Manager*, John Wiley & Sons Inc, New York, New York.

13   F. Wheen (2004) *How Mumbo Jumbo Conquered the World: a short history of modern delusions*, Harper Collins, London.

14   A. Robbins (1994) *Giant Steps: small changes to make a big difference*, Simon & Schuster UK Ltd, London.

15   http://www.marketresearch.com/product/display.asp?productid= 1338280&g=1.

16   F. Wheen (2004) *How Mumbo Jumbo Conquered the World: a short history of modern delusions* Harper Collins, London.

17   Carl Bernstein 'A Woman in Charge', cited in http://sweetness-light.com/archive/when-hillary-channeled-eleanor-roosevelt.

18   http://sweetness-light.com/archive/when-hillary-channeled-eleanor-roosevelt.

19   H. G. Frankfurt (2005) *On Bullshit*, Princeton University Press, Princeton, New Jersey.

20 J. Whyte (2003) *Bad Thoughts: a guide to clear thinking*, Corvo Books Ltd, London.

21 J. Hogg, (1970) *The Private Memoirs and Confessions of a Justified Sinner*, Oxford University Press, Oxford: http://www.timesonline.co.uk/tol/news/politics/article7032217.ece.

22 CIPD, 2006 Training and Development Survey, CIPD, London.

23 M. Higgs, 'Narcissistic Leadership', *Journal of Change Management*, June 2009.

24 S. Davis, J. Lukomnik, D. Pitt-Watson (2006) *The New Capitalists*, Harvard Business School Press, Boston, Mass.

25 L. Festinger (1957) *A Theory of Cognitive Dissonance*, Row & Peterson, Illinois.

26 R. L. Martin (2003) *The Responsibility Virus*, Pearson Education Limited, Harlow, UK.

CHAPTER TWO

1 This is a tribute to the marketing genius of L'Oreal in capturing the spirit of the age with their strap line reflecting the increasing importance of looking after oneself.

2 Tipping Point or Falling Down? Democracy and the British General Election 2010. Sourced from http://www.cultdyn.co.uk/ART067736u/democracy2010.html.

3 http://www.cultdyn.co.uk/ART067736u/Now_People_0.pdf.

4 Dictionary.com, 'lifestyle,' in The American Heritage® Dictionary of the English Language, Fourth Edition. Source location: Houghton Mifflin Company, 2004. http://dictionary.reference.com/browse/lifestyle. Available: http://dictionary.reference.com.

5 *The Oxford Dictionary of Current English* (2009) Oxford University Press, Oxford. (http://www.encyclopedia.com/The+Oxford+Pocket+Dictionary+of+Current+English/publications.aspx?date=200607&pageNumber=168).

6   M. Gladwell, 'The Talent Myth: are smart people overrated?' *The New Yorker*, July 2002.

7   See R. Hogan, R. Raskin, D. Fazzini, (1990) 'The dark side of charisma'. In K. Clark, M. Clark (eds), *Measures of Leadership* (pp. 343–354). West Orange, NJ: Leadership Library of America.

8   G. Hamel (2002) *Leading the Revolution*, Harvard Business School Press, Boston, Mass.

9   For a wonderfully vivid description of Tulipomania see C. McKay (1852) *Memoirs of Extraordinary Popular Delusions and the Madness of Crowds*, Office of the National Illustrated Library, London which has a whole chapter on this and the other early speculations referred to in this chapter. It can be see on google books and is still in print today.

10 E. N. Williams (1980) *The Penguin Dictionary of English and European History*, Penguin, Harmondsworth, UK.

11 See D. Marshall (1962) *Eighteenth Century England*, Longman, London pp. 121–129 for a summary of the South Sea Bubble.

12 http://www.4wheelsnews.com/report-funds-sue-porsche-for-fraud-over-volkswagen/; accessed 3 August 2010.

13 'The Great CEO Pay Race: Over Before It Begins', Canadian Centre for Policy Alternatives, December 2007.

14 'Big Paychecks', Forbes.com, March 2007.

15 http://www.webpronews.com/expertarticles/2007/01/03.

16 Economic & Social Research Council (2005) *Seven Deadly Sins: a new look at society through an old lens*, ESRC.

17 P. Pope, S. Young (2002) *Executive Remuneration: an investor's guide*, International Centre for Research in Accounting, Lancaster University.

18 Quoted in S. Davis, J. Lukomnik, D. Pitt-Watson (2006) *The New Capitalists*, Harvard Business School Press, 2006.

19 J. Heller (1974, 1997) (Scribner paperback edition) *Something Happened*, Simon & Schuster, New York.

20   R. B. Kaiser, R. Hogan (2006) 'The Dark Side of Discretion' Research Report, Hogan Assessment Systems.

21   G. Hegel (1956) *The Philosophy of History*, Dover Publications.

22   *Oxford Dictionary of Quotations* (1975) Oxford University Press, London.

23   Several 'new' CEO packages have come under serious criticism recently for not recognizing public disquiet about top executive pay.

24   Banking Crisis: reforming corporate governance and pay in the City, House of Commons Treasury Committee, Ninth Report of Session 2008–09, 12 May 2009

25   http://www.telegraph.co.uk/finance/jobs/7728860/Executive-Pay-Report-2010-How-the-recession-has-reshaped-boardroom-pay.html.

26   http://www.telegraph.co.uk/finance/newsbysector/retailand consumer/7036463/Warren-Buffett-Krafts-11.9bn-takeover-of-Cadbury-is-a-bad-deal.html.

27   There is a huge body of work in this area, but in the light of this chapter a good starting point would be http://www.fma.org/Hamburg/Papers/CEOvaluedestruction.pdf: Liu, Taffler & John (2009) 'CEO Value Destruction in M&A Deals and Beyond', Financial Management Association Conference Paper, Hamburg as an example of the many studies linking value destruction to CEO behaviour.

CHAPTER THREE

1   http://www.dailymail.co.uk/news/article-1083290/Its-awful–Why-did-coming–The-Queen-gives-verdict-global-credit-crunch.html.

2   'What it takes to restore trust in business' HBS Working Knowledge, 5 May 2003, http://hbswk.hbs.edu/item/3456.html.

3   British Venture Capital Association 'Why private equity is good for the UK', http://www.bvca.co.uk.

4   *Business Week* 29 May 2007, 'Private Equity's Big Debt Burden' http://www.businessweek.com/bwdaily/dnflash/content/may2007/db20070529_241277.htm.

5   For the most recent rescue see http://www.reuters.com/article/idUSTRE4AJ45G20081124; the reference to the 1970s rescue came from: http://www.leftbusinessobserver.com/HowToDefault.html.

6   *Business Week* 29 May 2007, 'Private Equity's Big Debt Burden' http://www.businessweek.com/bwdaily/dnflash/content/may2007/db20070529_241277.htm.

7   http://users.powernet.co.uk/hack/sleaze/.

8   http://www.telegraph.co.uk/news/newstopics/politics/labour/3179722/The-Ecclestone-Affair-Labours-first-funding-scandal.html.

9   http://www.foe.co.uk/resource/press_releases/0601tors.html.

10 http://www.insidehighered.com/news/2007/09/17/mba.

11 N. Ferguson (2010) 'Men, Money & Morality: How Can Trust in Banking Be Restored?' public lecture, 6 July St Paul's Cathedral, London.

12 In 2007, for example, Barclays Bank PLC's retail operations contributed just 17.1% of its overall profitability whilst its investment operations (Barclays Capital) contributed 31.2%. http://group.barclays.com/Investor-Relations/Financial-results-and-publications/Results-announcements?tab=122580291669.

13 http://www.creditaction.org.uk/debt-statistics/2010/february-2010.html.

14 http://www1.landregistry.gov.uk/houseprices/housepriceindex/report/default.asp?step=4&locationType=0&area=E%26W-ALL&reporttype=1&datetype=1&from1=01%2F2007&from2=01%2F2010&image2.x=31&image2.y=14.

15 The bank's repossession rate rose by 63% in 2008 over 2007. Sourced from: http://www.telegraph.co.uk/finance/newsbysector/

banksandfinance/4931011/Northern-Rock-repossessions-jump.
html.

16 http://news.findlaw.com/hdocs/docs/aig/exec-bonuses-cuomo
31709ltr.html.

17 P. F. Drucker (1985) *Entrepreneurship and Innovation*, Butterworth-
Heinemann, Oxford. Reference taken from Classic Drucker
Collection edition with Foreword by C. J. Bones (2007).

18 S. Davis, J. Lukomnik, D. Pitt-Watson (2006) *The New Capitalists*,
Harvard Business School Press, Boston Mass.

19 B. G. Malkiel, A Saha (undated) 'Hedge Funds: Risk and Return'
http://www.princeton.edu/~bmalkiel/Global%20Hedge%20
fund%20NEW.pdf.

20 Wikipedia cites Robert W. Hamilton (1995) 'Registered
Limited Liability Partnerships: Present at Birth (Nearly)',
Colorado Law Review 66: 1065, 1069. as a source for the US
history.

21 http://www.bytestart.co.uk/content/19/19_1/set-up-a-limited-
liability-partnership.shtml.

22 http://www.bondpearce.com/Partnerships.

CHAPTER FOUR

1 Two good examples are Naomi Klein (2007) *The Shock Doctrine*,
Metropolitan Books/Henry Holt and Raj Patel (2009) *The Value
of Nothing*, Portobello Books, London.

2 An interesting summary of statistics that reinforce this point can be
found at: http://www.theworldeconomy.org/.

3 http://www.guardian.co.uk/world/2009/apr/14/cuba-us-sanct
ions-obama.

4 K. MacMillan, K. Money, S. Downing, C. Hillenbrand (2004)
'Giving your organization SPIRIT' *Journal of General Management*,
Vol. 30.

5   K. Money (2009) 'Rebuilding Trust' in *The Henley Manifesto*, Henley Business School, Reading, UK.

6   S. Davis, J. Lukomnik, D. Pitt-Watson (2006) *The New Capitalists*, Harvard Business School Press, Boston, Mass.

7   See, e.g. A. Sargeant, S. Lee (2002) 'Improving public trust in the voluntary sector: An empirical analysis', *International Journal of Non-Profit and Voluntary Sector Marketing*, Vol. 7, No. 1.

8   S. Lee S (2009) 'Trust and Confidence' in *The Henley Manifesto*, Henley Business School, Reading, UK.

9   The leading proponents of Economic Value Added were Stern Stewart & Co whose proposition is that they have taken business economics from the classroom to the boardroom. Their thesis can be found at http://www.qfinance.com/business-strategy-best-practice/why-eva-is-the-best-measurement-tool-for-creating-share holder-value?full.

10   The leading consultants in the field were Marakon Associates and their theory and approach, from which this summary is derived is contained in: J. McTaggart, P. Kontes, M. Mankins (1994) *The Value Imperative*, The Free Press, New York, New York.

11   A. Smith (1776), *An Inquiry into the Nature and Causes of the Wealth of Nations by Adam Smith*, edited with an Introduction, Notes, Marginal Summary and an Enlarged Index by Edwin Cannan (London: Methuen, 1904): 'By preferring the support of domestic to that of foreign industry, he intends only his own security; and by directing that industry in such a manner as its produce may be of the greatest value, he intends only his own gain, and he is in this, as in many other cases, led by an invisible hand to promote an end which was no part of his intention'. Vol. 1: chapter ii: of restraints upon the importation from foreign countries of such goods as can be produced at home: http://oll.libertyfund.org/title/237/212333/3427065.

12 J. McTaggart, P. Kontes, M. Mankins (1994) *The Value Imperative*, The Free Press, New York, New York, defines the equation as $V = B \times ROE\text{-}g/Ke\text{-}g$ where V = Equity value of common stock; B = Beginning book value of equity investment; ROE = Expected long-term return on equity; g = Expected long-term growth in equity ($\geq$GNP growth) and Ke = Cost of equity capital. A test will be held at the end of the chapter.

13 P. J. O'Rourke (1998) *Eat The Rich*, Atlantic Monthly Press, New York, New York.

14 H. A. Miskimin (1967) 'Two Reforms of Charlemagne? Weights and Measures in the Middle Ages', Harry A. Miskimin, *The Economic History Review*, New Series, Vol. 20, No. 1 (Apr.), pp. 35–52, published by: Blackwell Publishing on behalf of the Economic History Society URL: http://www.jstor.org/stable/2592034.

CHAPTER FIVE

1 http://www.walesonline.co.uk/business-in-wales/business-news/2010/03/10/barclays-chief-attacks-tax-changes-91466-25998191/.

2 Of the 100 largest economies in the world in 2000, fifty-one were corporations; only forty-nine were countries (based on a comparison of corporate sales and country GDPs) sourced from: http://www.corpwatch.org/article.php?id=377.

CHAPTER SIX

1 For one example of the importance of looking at your boots in diamond prospecting see: http://www.mwadui.com/Mwadui/Mwadui_15.htm.

2 http://autoassembly.mckinsey.com/html/downloads/articles/War_For_Talent.pdf.

3   See K. Eichenwald, (2005) *Conspiracy of Fools: a true story*, Broadway Books, New York, New York and 'Ford ignored its human needs, now it's paying', Automotive News 77 (2 August, 2002) as two often cited assessments of the impact of the McKinsey approach.

4   E. Michaels, H. Handfield-Jones, B. Axelrod (2001) *The War For Talent*, Harvard Business School Press, Boston, Mass.

5   C. J. Bones (2007) 'Engagement is at the heart of successful M&A', *Ivey Business Journal* January/February, Richard Ivey School of Business, London, Ontario.

6   http://www.gallup.com/consulting/52/employee-engagement. aspx.

7   D. Sirota, L. A. Mischkind, M. I. Seltzer (2005) *The Enthusiastic Employee*, Wharton School Publishing, New Jersey.

8   http://autoassembly.mckinsey.com/html/downloads/articles/ War_For_Talent.pdf.

9   I understand from colleagues at Cadbury during subsequent surveys that this remained the case.

10 D. Sirota, L. A. Mischkind, M. I. Seltzer (2005) *The Enthusiastic Employee*, Wharton School Publishing, New Jersey.

11 http://www.usatoday.com/money/economy/employment/2005-03-13-fired-usat_x.htm.

12 For the twelve questions see: http://www.workforce.com/section/ 09/article/23/53/40.html.

13 http://news.bbc.co.uk/1/hi/uk/1657826.stm.

14 *The New Rules of Engagement*, Chartered Institute of Personnel & Development, London 2004.

15 *Working in the 21st Century*, The Tomorrow Project, London 2005.

16 *Managing Tomorrow's Worker*, Future of Work Forum, Henley Business School (2005) Henley-on-Thames, UK.

17 *Working in the 21st Century*, The Tomorrow Project, London 2005.

18 J. Collins, J. I. Porras (2002) *Built to Last*, Harper Business Essentials.

19   http://www.jimcollins.com/article_topics/articles/good-to-great. html.

20   See http://www.fastcompany.com/magazine/04/hiring.html as one of many articles reflecting on successful company practices based on this approach.

21   http://www.growingbusiness.co.uk/performance-or-attitude-what-s-more-important.html.

22   S. G. Barsade (2000) 'The Ripple Effect: emotional contagion in groups' (October). Yale SOM Working Paper No. OB-01. Available at SSRN: http://ssrn.com/abstract=250894 or doi:10.2139/ ssrn.250894.

23   L. M. Bradley, (2006) 'Perceptions of justice when selecting internal and external job candidates', *Personnel Review*, Vol. 35 Iss. 1, pp. 66–77.

24   P. Martins, F. Lima (2006) *Applied Economics Letters*, 1466–4291, Vol. 13, Iss: 14.

25   F. Herzberg, B. Mausner, B. Bloch Snyderman (1959) *The Motivation to Work*, John Wiley & Sons Inc, New York.

26   Survey cited on http://www.businessballs.com/herzberg.htm.

27   http://www.employment-studies.co.uk/pubs/summary.php?id =334: M. T. Strebler, D. Robinson, P. Heron (1997) Report 334, Institute for Employment Studies, June.

CHAPTER SEVEN

1   J. K. Galbraith (1980) *Annals of an Abiding Liberal*, Andre Deutsch, New York, New York.

2   A. Cadbury (1992) *Report of the Committee on the Financial Aspects of Corporate Governance*, Gee, London.

3   R. Greenbury (1995). *Directors Remuneration: Report of a Study Group Chaired by Sir Richard Greenbury*, Gee, London. This report is one of the most important contributions to this issue. Adopted by the UK's London Stock Exchange as a requirement for listing, it

lays down strong principles which have been more honoured in the breach rather than in the observance. It can be found at: http://www.ecgi.org/codes/code.php?code_id=131.

4   D. Higgs (2003) *Review of the Role and Effectiveness of Non-executive Directors*, The Department of Trade and Industry, London.

5   D. Bolchover (2010) *Pay Check*, Coptic Publishing, London, quoting research done by the AFL-CIO in 2005.

6   L. Bebchuck, Y. Grinstein (2005) 'The Growth of Executive Pay', *Oxford Review of Economic Policy*, Vol. 21, No. 2.

7   P. Hodgson, R. Marshall, 'Pay for Failure: The Compensation Committees Responsible', The Corporate Library, June 2006. See: http://www.thecorporatelibrary.com/tcl-store/PressReleases/865mm_in_ceo_compensation_while.htm cited in 'CEO Pay Reform: A Point/Counterpoint' (http://www.corporatepolicy.org/pdf/CEO_Pay_Point_Counterpoint.pdf).

8   http://www.thecorporatelibrary.com/news_docs/28050707 payforfailureii.pdf.

9   The US market offered significantly higher returns for stocks, bonds and bills over the final twenty-five years than over the first seventy-five years. Source: http://www.cxoadvisory.com/big-ideas/triumph-of-the-optimists-chapter-by-chapter-review/.

10 http://www.ft.com/cms/s/2/412d1354-ffd6-11de-ad8c-00144 feabdc0,dwp_uuid=91a27406-05c5-11df-88ee-00144feabdc0. html.

11 P. Drucker (1959) *Landmarks of Tomorrow: a report on the new 'postmodern world*, Harper & Brothers, New York, New York.

12 D. Bolchover (2010) *Pay Check*, Coptic Publishing, London: the figure cited is that for Stan O'Neil, former CEO of Merrill Lynch who between 2003–2006 earned $145 million: about $100,000 a day.

13 CIPD (2010) *Transforming Public Sector Pay and Pensions*, CIPD Publications, London.

14 http://www.salarytrack.co.uk/average-graduate-salary.html.

15   CIPD (2010) *Reward Management 2010*, CIPD Publications, London.

16   http://hilltop.bradley.edu/~arr/bsm/pg04.html.

17   P. J. O'Rourke (1998) *Eat the Rich*, Atlantic Monthly Press, New York, New York.

18   http://news.bbc.co.uk/1/hi/business/8243828.stm.

19   http://www.neweconomics.org/sites/neweconomics.org/files/Behavioural_Economics_1.pdf.

20   http://www.leadershipconsulting.com/evidence-based-management-the-science-side-of-motivation.htm.

21   R. M. Hayes, S. Schaefer (2008) 'CEO Pay and the Lake Wobegon Effect'; sourced from http://papers.ssrn.com/sol3/papers.cfm?abstract_id=966332.

CHAPTER EIGHT

1   H. Mintzberg, (2006) *Financial Times*, 23 October 2006.

2   S. N. Kaplan, B. A. Minton (2008) 'How has CEO Turnover Changed' sourced from: http://faculty.chicagobooth.edu/steven.kaplan/research/km.pdf.

3   http://www.samallen.co.uk/downloads/FTSE%20250%20CEOs.pdf.

4   D. A. Heenan, W. Bennis (1999) *Co-Leaders: the power of great partnerships*, John Wiley & Sons Inc, New York, New York.

5   D. A. Heenan, W. Bennis (1999) *Co-Leaders: the power of great partnerships*, John Wiley & Sons Inc, New York, New York.

6   R. Goffee, G. Jones (2006) 'Why should Anyone Be Led by you?: What It Takes To Be an Authentic Leader'.

7   A model developed by John Adair in the 1970s that was the first to look at leadership as an activity that could be broken down and taught.

8   The leading proponents of this are Paul Hersey and Ken Blanchard.

9 E. Schein (1988) 'Organizational Culture' MIT Working paper 2088-88 sourced from: http://dspace.mit.edu/bitstream/handle/1721.1/2224/SWP-2088-24854366.pdf?sequence=1.

10 An interesting article on the importance of engagement with change to deliver changed outcomes is D. Rock, J. Schwartz (2006) 'The Neuroscience of Leadership'. *Strategy+Business*, Vol. 43. This explores and challenges some of the more traditional methods of change management and stresses the importance of focused attention in individuals as a driver for achieving sustained personal change.

11 D. Ulrich, N. Smallwood (2007) *Leadership Brand: developing customer-focused leaders to drive performance and lasting value*, Harvard Business School Press, Boston, Mass.

12 A good example is: C. Kelly, P. Kocourek, N. McGaw, J. Samuelson (2005) Deriving Value from Corporate Values, The Aspen Institute and Booz Allen Hamilton. Available at www.aspeninstitute.org/publications/deriving-value-corporate-values.

13 http://specials.ft.com/enron/FT3L4NIOSZC.html.

14 R. Moss Kanter (2009). *SuperCorp: how vanguard companies create innovation, profits, growth, and social good*, Crown Business, Harmondsworth, Middlesex.

15 The Inner Game series originated with 'The Inner Game of Tennis' by Timothy Gallwey and has spawned many related books and articles. The coaching book that best outlines the approach is by John Whitmore (1992) *Coaching for Performance*, Nicholas Brealey Publishing, London, UK.

CONCLUSION

1 O. Wilde (1893) *Lady Windermere's Fan*, Penguin Popular Classics.

2 R. Patel (2009) *The Value of Nothing*, Portobello Books, London. Interestingly Patel attributes the Wilde quotation to *The Picture of Dorian Gray* for which I can find no corroboration

and fails to position it as a very insightful answer to the question: 'What is a cynic?' Wilde's point is mine today: a belief in the value of the greater good is always at risk from those who cynically use their power and influence for their own advantage. Ensuring that leaders meet Aristotle's requirement for 'virtue' is critical in any democracy. Whilst Patel uses the quotation to condemn consumerism (into which he argues we have been forced) he misses the point about the consumer proposition. It is about meeting what we value with products and services at a price we are prepared to purchase – even if the price we pay includes borrowing to be able to afford it. Good government protects people who don't appreciate the impact of their decisions from themselves, just as much as it should protect them from the unscrupulous. This is the argument for the re-introduction of much stricter controls over the access to credit, for example, which would automatically realign consumer behaviour with the reality of managing the world's scarce resources.

3   D. Prosser (2010) 'The Dizzy Heights', *The Independent*, 15 June 2010.

4   *Climate Change – Who Cares?* AIESEC International Publications, December 2009.

5   In February 1968 Warhol exhibited his first international retrospective exhibition at the Moderna Museet gallery in Stockholm. The exhibition catalogue contained 'In the future everybody will be world famous for fifteen minutes.' Sourced from: http://www.phrases.org.uk/meanings/fifteen-minutes-of-fame.html.

6   R. A. Heifetz, M. Linksy (2002) *Leadership on the Line*, quoted in http://www.cambridge-leadership.com/publications/pdfs/Heifetz_LOTL.pdf.

Index

360 degree feedback
    surveys 28–9, 148
ABN-AMRO 8
'above average performance',
    concepts 112–14
accountabilities 219–28
accountants 94–5
achievement, concepts 27–30,
    143–5, 155–6
'Action Centred Leadership' 209
activists/campaigners against
    globalization 119–20, 230–1
Acton, Lord 62
Adams Inc. 141–2
adaptive change, concepts 237–9
Adenauer, Konrad 207
Adler, Alfred 4
advancement opportunities,
    Herzberg model 155–6
advertisements 46, 47–66
Africa 10, 75
AIESEC 236
AIG 87–8, 215
Al Quaeda 74
alignment benefits, concepts 139–40,
    203–4, 227–8

Alltel deal 72
'altruistic' leaders 8–9
Amazon 5–6, 26
annual general meetings
    (AGMs) 92–3, 129, 168
annual performance
    reviews 28–9, 148, 157–63,
    178–9, 190–1
antinomianism 35
appointments
    leaders 16–17, 79, 130–1,
    137–8, 170–2
    non-executive directors 130–1,
    167–8, 228
The Apprentice (tv series) 47
arbitrage houses 52–3
Aristotle 8–9, 18, 23–4, 31,
    61–2, 77–8
Arnault, Bernard 7
art history 16–23
Arthurian legends, art history 18
Asia 75
aspirations, critique 2–4, 8,
    100–1
asset values, short-term
    changes 2, 73–4

asymmetrical information 183–4,
    197
Attila the Hun 31
attitude factors, concepts 150–1,
    158–60, 227–8
audits 39–40, 94–5, 129–30,
    234, 238–9
Australia, executive rewards 57
authentic business
    concepts 121–3, 127–35,
        210–28, 233–9
    definition 233–4

bad leaders 7–8, 10–12, 39–40,
    58–60, 61–2
Bad Thoughts (Whyte) 34
balanced scorecards 161
bankruptcies 59–60, 64, 85–6,
    94–5, 146, 166–7, 230
banks
    call centres 113–14, 212
    capital adequacy
        requirements 92
    confidence crisis 110
    credit boom 2–4, 67–74, 80–97
    critique 2–3, 8, 25, 36–7,
        52–3, 54–5, 63–4, 67–9,
        72–3, 80–8, 110, 127–8,
        174–5, 229–39
    deregulated financial
        services 80–8, 92–3, 117–18
    executive rewards 63–4,
        69–74, 82–3, 86–8, 127–8

lessons not learned 63–4,
    67–8, 87–8, 127–8, 174–5
misperceptions 63–4, 67–8,
    87–8, 127–8, 174–5
reform needs 64–5, 72–4,
    96–7, 100–1, 229–30
rescue packages 73, 87–8,
    106–7, 127–8
Barclays 8
Barton, Joey 4
BBC 76, 106
'Because You're Worth It'
    advertisement 46
behavioural economists 198–9,
    204–8
Belbin, Meredith 27
beliefs
    concepts 108–10, 114–23,
        198–9, 211–28
    trust concepts 108–10
belonging and acceptance, human
    needs/wants 37–8
benchmarking 32, 111–14,
    190–1, 200–1, 204–6
benefits
    concepts 188, 195, 228
Berkshire Hathaway 208
Berlusconi, Silvio 4, 25
Big Brother (tv series) 47
billionaires, celebrity cultures 5
Black, Conrad 4
Black-Scholes options pricing
    model 182–3

Blair, Tony 2, 4–5, 22, 25, 33, 62, 76

blame cultures 1–2, 5–6, 42–3

Blankfien, Lloyd 4

boards of directors 127–8, 204–5, 215, 217–19, 224–5, 227–8, 235–6

roles 217–19, 227, 235–6

solutions 215, 217–19, 224–5, 227–8, 235–6

Bondone, Giotto Di 17

bonuses

concepts 180–1, 192–3, 196

critique 53–4, 55–6, 63–4, 127–8, 176–7, 180–1, 192–3, 196, 238–9

retained amounts 193

solutions 192–3, 196, 238–9

teams 192–3, 223

Booth, Cherie 33

Botticelli, Sandro 17–18

Bourbons 19

Boyatzis, Robert 27–8

BP 132–3, 230, 232

brands, critique 212–15, 220, 222, 225

Branson, Sir Richard 7

Brazil

middle class consumption 100

trust surveys 11

British Values Survey 45–6

Brown, Gordon 5

Browne, Lord 7

BSkyB 76–7

bubbles 50–4, 71–4

Buffet, Warren 66

building societies 82–8

bullies 39

'bullshit' 33–4

Bush, George W. 2

business

critique 1–2

society conflicts 70–1, 75–80, 132, 174–5, 189, 220–2, 228, 229–39

business books

leadership gurus 31–5, 208–28

statistics 5–6, 25–6, 32

business gods, 'gods' that failed 4–5, 7–8, 25, 67–8, 122–3, 206–7, 227–8

business schools 26, 50, 60, 77–9, 135, 171–2

'case study' approaches 78–9

critique 77–9, 135, 171–2

'ethical oath' 79–80

research and publish drives 26

Business Week 71–3

Cadbury Code 166–7

Cadbury Schweppes 65–6, 141–3, 224–5

the Caesars, art history 18

call centres, banks 113–14, 212

camaraderie, engagement drivers 143–5

campaigners against globalization 119–20

Canada, executive rewards 55–6

capital adequacy requirements, banks 92

capital gods, 'gods' that failed 4

capital growth 53, 67–8, 111–14, 231–2

capital markets
critique 67–97, 98
flows 52–3

capitalism 39–40, 98, 105–6, 170–1, 229–39

Caplin, Carole 4, 33

caps, executive rewards 196, 201

'case study' approaches, business schools 78–9

Catch 22, Something Happened (Heller) 58–9

celebrity cultures, critique 2–5, 7–8, 59–60, 149, 206–7, 208–28, 232–3, 236–9

CEOs 7–8, 25, 40, 55–7, 70–4, 78, 86–8, 122–3, 149, 167–8, 174–5, 196, 200–1, 206–28, 232–7
company rankings 7–8, 78
'Lake Wobegon Effect' 200–1, 236–7
turnover statistics 206

chairmen, solutions 218–19

change 12, 64–5, 68–74, 96–7, 100–1, 118–23, 127–35, 136–45, 189–201, 208–28, 229–30, 233–9
adaptive change 237–9
cultural issues 118–23, 141–3, 208–28
difficulties 211–12, 237–9

characteristics of leaders 7–9, 10, 18–19, 21–2, 24–5, 27–30, 34–5, 108–10, 203–28, 233–9

Charlemagne (AD 742–814) 116

Charles I, King of England 19

Chaucer, Geoffrey 24, 30

China
middle class consumption 99
trust surveys 11

Chopra, Deepak 32

Christianity 6–7, 17–19, 67

Chrysler 208

churches, critique 70

Churchill dynasty 24

Churchill, Sir Winston 24, 207

Citigroup report (2007) 72–3

The City 81–2

civil ownership of capital 128–9, 228, 234–5

classical leadership discourses, concepts 23–6

climate change 1, 9, 119–20, 195, 236

Clinton, Bill 4, 32–3

Clinton, Hilary 32–3

co-leaders, concepts 208–9

the Co-op 83

coaching 156, 225, 226, 237–9

coalition government in the
    UK 77

codes of conduct 222

cold showers, warm gestures 189,
    201

collaborative approaches,
    solutions 128–35, 145–6,
    150–1, 192–3, 202–3, 207–28

collectivist cultures 100, 208–28

Collins, Jim 149

commercial banks 80–8

commitment
    concepts 139–40, 142–5,
        150–1, 221–8
    definition 140, 144

communication gods, 'gods' that
    failed 4

communication skills 28–30,
    36–8, 145–6, 149–50,
    218–19, 221–2, 223, 238–9

Companies Act 2006 96

competencies
    assessment problems 157–60,
        204–7
    leaders 27–30, 33–4, 109–10,
        122–3, 148, 157–60, 204–8,
        237–9
    role 159–60

competitive advantage,
    definition 112, 172–3, 220–2

competitive environments, impacts 80,
    88–94, 171, 220–2

computational failings,
    decision-making 199

conclusion 229–39

Confederation of British Industry
    (CBI) 65

confidence in leaders 1–2, 4–5,
    9–10, 12, 39–40, 101,
    104–5, 107–10, 116–17,
    121–3, 209–28, 229–39
    concepts 101, 104–5, 107–10,
        116–17, 121–3
    definition 108–9
    global financial crisis from
        2007 110
    public policy agendas 109–10

conflicts of interest 64–5, 69–74,
    89–97
    concepts 70–4
    leaders 64–5, 69–74, 89–97
    politics 70–4

conformity dangers, leaders 30,
    31–5, 236–9

Confucius 31

Conservative party 77, 84–5

consumption 2–7, 44–66, 80,
    99–100, 133–4, 173, 227,
    229–30
    critique 2–7, 44–66, 99–100,
        229–30
    'lifestyle' emergence 2–5,
        44–66, 80, 99–100

scarce resources 2, 99–100,
    133–4, 173, 227
core purpose of the
    organization 149, 162,
    202–3, 224–5, 227–8
corporate governance 64–5,
    69–71, 95–7, 106–7,
    128–35, 166–70, 181,
    215–28, 230–9
    Cadbury Code 166–7
    critique 96–7, 106–7, 128–9,
        215, 230–1
    executive rewards 64–5, 96,
        129–30, 167–8, 181
    Greenbury Report 167–8,
        193, 196
    Higgs Review 168
    reforms 64–5, 96–7, 128–35,
        166–70, 215–28
    Sarbanes-Oxley Act 2002 96
corruption 39–40, 62–3, 75–80,
    229–30
cosmetic enhancements, 'lifestyle'
    emergence 4, 44–5, 47–8,
    214
Covey, Stephen 32
'cracker mottoes' 31–2
creative accounting, Enron 50, 59
credit boom 2–4, 67–74, 80–97
credit cards 4
credit crunch *see* global financial
    crisis from 2007
credit defaults 72–4

crowns/sceptres/orbs/ermine
    state trappings, art
    history 18
Cuba 99–100
cults, critique 34–5
cultural issues 28–30, 34–5,
    37–8, 90–7, 99–101,
    112–14, 140–4, 147–8,
    152–3, 203–4, 208–28, 239
    change 118–23, 208–28
    commitment factors 140–5,
        150–1, 221–2
    definitions 118–19, 210–11
    internal/external recruitment
        candidates 152–3
customers 102–7, 113–14, 203,
    213, 234, 239
    high-value customers 113–14
    loyalties 103–7, 113–14, 203
    satisfaction issues 103–7,
        113–14, 203, 213
cynic, definition 229

'Darfur' 1
The Dark Side of Charisma
    (Hogan, Raskin and
    Fazzini) 49–50
Darwin, Charles 24
decentralization needs 38
decision-making
    behavioural economists 198–9,
        204–8
    human fears 41, 98–9, 198–9

investors 112–14, 128–35,
    198–9
leaders 49, 60, 140–1, 198–9,
    221–2, 224–5, 227–8
narcissists 49, 60
defined contribution retirement
    schemes 186–7
DeGaulle, Charles 25
deities, human forms 16, 17–19,
    23–4, 203–4, 206–7
Dell 169
demographic changes 145–6
deregulated financial services
    critique 2–3, 52, 54–5,
        66, 81–8, 92–4, 117–18,
        177
    failure 117–18
    historical background 81–8,
        92
    risk-free attitudes 81–8
despots 25
development issues
    leaders 15–26, 135, 142–3,
        147–8, 154–6, 164–5,
        209–28, 235–9
    line managers 164–5, 212–13
    organizational
        leadership 224–5, 233–9
    teams 224–5
    workforce 146–7, 154–6,
        164–5, 235–9
'diamonds on the soles of you
    shoes' 136–7

differentials, executive
    rewards 56, 96, 135, 168–9,
        174–5, 190–1, 192–3, 196,
        234–9
disclosures 69–71
discourses, leadership
    discourses 23–6
discretionary effort,
    engagement 141–8, 209
dishonest leaders 10, 69–70,
    230–9
dissenting voices 209, 223
diversity benefits 30, 159–60,
    202–3, 207–28, 237–9
donors, politics 70–1, 75–80, 134
'dotcom' bubble 52, 71–2
Drucker, Peter 89, 172–3
Durkheim, Emile 24
dynasties, leaders 18, 24–5

Eat the Rich (O'Rourke) 114–15
eBay 116–17
EBITDA 72
Ecclestone, Bernie 76
economic depressions 51
economic growth 2–4, 99–100,
    145, 169–70
economic liberalization, Thatcher
    governments 84–5
Economic Policy Institute 57
economic profit (EP)
    concepts 111–14, 224–5
    critique 113

definition 111

economic recessions 86–8

economic theory 170–5, 198–9

economic value added (EVA)

concepts 111–14, 224–5

critique 113

definition 111

economics gods, 'gods' that
failed 4

Edelman Trust Barometer 11

education systems

ethical values 7, 77, 79–80

leaders 135, 147, 224–5, 236

religious traditions 7

egoistic aspects of leaders 7–8,
11–12, 138–40, 202–3

the elect, leaders 34–5

Elizabeth I, Queen of
England 31

Elizabeth II, Queen of
England 69

emails 162

emotional abilities 28–30, 139–40

emotions towards businesses,
stakeholders 102–3

employees see workforce

employment contracts,
critique 154–6

empowerment 231–2

En-lai, Chou 208

engagement

concepts 139–48, 150–1,
155–6, 209–28

definition 140–1, 144–5

drivers 143–5, 146, 150–1,
155, 221–2

line managers 142–5, 161–3

enlightened autocrats, politics 25

The Enlightenment 20–1

Enron 25, 48–50, 58–9, 76, 96,
147, 188, 220, 230

creative accounting 50, 59

narcissists 49–50, 58–9

political donations 76

self-promotion aspects 49–50

entrepreneurs

concepts 89–97, 217–19

definition 89–90

risk attitudes 89–90

stewardship distinctions 90–1,
96, 217–19, 232, 239

environmental concerns 105–7,
109, 192–3, 221–2, 229–30,
234–6

environmental issues, leaders 15,
44–66, 67–97, 169–70

EP see economic profit

equity

engagement drivers 143–5

executive rewards 174–5

Ernst & Young 40

'ethical oath', business
schools 79–80

ethical values

education systems 7, 77,
79–80

leaders 10, 39–40, 60–1, 63,
    70–4, 121–3, 144–5,
    198–9, 203–28, 230–9
'Voice of the People' survey
    (2008) 10
Europe 2–5, 17–19, 25, 75, 77,
    87, 90–1, 110, 150–1,
    169–70, 181, 186–7,
    217–18, 226
  elected autocrats 25
  'lifestyle' emergence 2–5
  private equity houses 71
EVA *see* economic value added
evil, concepts 61–3, 123
executive rewards 48–50, 54–7,
    60–1, 63–4, 69–74, 82–3,
    86–8, 96–7, 107, 112–13,
    127–8, 135, 166–201, 222,
    234, 238–9
  AIG 87–8, 215
  banks 63–4, 69–74, 82–3,
    86–8, 127–8
  benefits 188, 195, 228
  caps 196, 201
  corporate governance 64–5,
    96, 129–30, 167–8, 181
  differentials 56, 96,
    135, 168–9, 174–5,
    190–1, 192–3, 196,
    234–9
  equity 174–5
  international
    comparisons 57–8

'Lake Wobegon Effect' 200–1,
    236–7
'market-based'
    approaches 176–9, 229–39
narcissists 55–6, 58, 60–1
performance issues 56–7,
    82–3, 135, 168–70, 178–81,
    190–1, 192–3, 199, 200–1,
    222, 234
reform needs 189–201
regulators 166–70, 238–9
relativity principle 196, 235
remuneration reports 64–5, 96,
    129–30, 167–70, 191, 194
retirement schemes 186–7
risk-free attitudes 65–6, 82–3,
    86–8, 185
salary/options proportion 56
'Say on Pay' legislation 167–8
scarce resources 173–5
share options 40, 55–7,
    182–5, 194, 201
shareholder activism 64–5,
    167–8
solutions 135, 189–201, 227,
    235–9
statistics 55–8, 168–9,
    176–80, 190–4
talent wars 48–50, 54–6,
    63–4, 135, 168–70, 171–9,
    200–1, 232–9
expenses, critique 35, 188, 195,
    214–15

external individual personal
    effectiveness programmes 226
Exxon-Mobil 53

fads/fashions 32, 50–1, 161–3,
    204
failure reasons, leaders 122–3,
    146, 203–4, 206–7, 238–9
fair trade, concepts 115–17
faith
    of Job 67–8
    trading instincts 116
'father or mother of the nation'
    symbolism, art history 19, 23
Ferguson, Niall 79
feudal-court analogy,
    organizations 7, 23
film stars, celebrity cultures 5,
    59–60, 236
final salary retirement
    schemes 186–7
Financial Services Agency 130–1
financial services industry
    confidence crisis 110
    critique 1, 2–3, 5, 8–11, 52–3,
        80–97, 110, 147–8
    Thatcher's economic
        liberalization 84–5
Financial Times 171–2
'the financial year' 192–3
Fiorina, Carly 4
FitzGerald, Niall 7
Florence, art history 17–18

followers, leaders 122–3,
    209–10, 237–9
Ford 169
France 11, 25, 51, 57, 73, 146
Frankfurt, Harry G. 33
free markets 11–12, 60–1, 98–9,
    170–5, 229–39
Freud, Sigmund 24, 30
Friedman, Milton 4
FTSE indices 206, 233
fund managers
    critique 52–4, 59, 65, 92–3,
        129, 134–5, 197, 239
    solutions 129, 134–5, 197,
        239

G20 131–2
Galbraith, J.K. 166, 168, 169
Gallup surveys 9–10
general elections 46
General Motors 31
Germanic legends, art history 18
Germany
    executive rewards 57
    trust surveys 10, 11
    Volkswagen (VW) 53–4
Gandhi, Mahatma 31, 33
Giant Steps (Robbins) 32
Gingrich, Newt 41–2
Gladwell, Malcolm 48–9, 136,
    138
global financial crisis from
    2007 1, 5, 9–11, 25, 33,

36–7, 48–50, 51–4, 58, 63,
67–74, 80–97, 106–7, 110,
117–18, 127–8, 218, 230
causes 69–74, 80–97, 127–8,
218
confidence crisis 110
statistics 84–5
warnings 69–74
globalization
activists/campaigners against
globalization 119–20,
230–1
concepts 9–10, 37–8, 52–3,
95–6, 119–20, 131–2,
231–9
G20 reforms 131–2
sizes of organizations 131–5
God 17–19, 23–4, 35, 74
'gods' that failed 1–12, 15–16,
25–6, 67–8, 117–18,
122–3, 206–7, 227–8
business gods 4–5, 7–8, 25,
67–8, 122–3, 206–7, 227–8
list 4, 7–8
penalties 5
Goffee, Rob 209–10
Goldman Sachs 230
good and evil, concepts 61–3,
123, 214–15, 238–9
good leaders 1, 26, 27–30, 61–2,
207–8, 233–9
goods and services,
value-creation 2

Goodwin, Sir Fred 4, 35, 63
governments 1–2, 102–7,
119–20, 127–35
critique 1–2, 119–20, 127–35
public policy agendas 109–10,
118–20, 122–3, 127–35,
159–60, 228
graduates, salaries 178
Great Britain
income-distribution
statistics 2–4
'lifestyle' emergence 2–5, 7–8
'greater good' 61–2, 119–20
Greco-Roman local mythology,
art history 18
greedy private equity
houses 71–2
Greek philosophers 8–9, 74
Greenbury Report 167–8, 193,
196
Greenspan, Alan 4
gross domestic product 2
'the guiding hand' of Adam
Smith 115
Gulf of Mexico oil rig
explosion 132–3, 232

habits 198–9
Hamel, Gary 50
Hapsburgs 19
Harvard Business School 69, 78
Harvey-Jones, Sir John 7
Hayes, Rachel M. 200–1

Hayward, Tony 132–3
health insurance benefits 195
hedge funds 52–4, 87, 92–3
Hegel, Georg Wilhelm
    Friedrich 42, 61–3, 123,
    214–15
Heifetz, Ronald 237–8
Heller, Joseph 58–9
Henley Business School 27
heroic leaders, critique 41–2,
    208–28
Herzberg, F 154–5
Hickel, Joseph (AD 1736–1807)
    20
Higgs, Malcolm 23, 39, 168
Higgs Review, corporate
    governance 168
high-value customers,
    banks 113–14
historical background on
    leadership 15–43, 231–2
HIV/AIDS 120
Hogg, James 35
Hohenzollerns 19
Hollinger 230
Holy Roman Empire 116
home workers 145–6
Homer 24, 90
honesty 10, 69–70, 230–9
house prices 85–8, 169–70
Houston, Jean 32–3
How Mumbo Jumbo Conquered the
    World (Wheen) 31–2

HP 4
human forms, deities 16, 17–19,
    23–4, 203–4, 206–7
human needs/wants 37–8, 41–3,
    98–123, 198–9, 202–3, 228,
    237–9
    belonging and
        acceptance 37–8
    leaders 41–3, 98–9, 122–3,
        198–9, 202–3, 228, 237–9
    leadership needs 41–3, 98–9,
        122–3, 202–3, 228, 237–9
    public wants 41–3, 98–123,
        202–3, 228, 237–9
    trading instincts 114–16
Human Resources (HR),
    critique 29–30, 36–7,
    161–3, 204–5, 212
human weaknesses 6–7, 12,
    29–30, 50–1, 157–60,
    213–15, 237–9
humanity-improvement aims,
    leaders 38, 60–1, 189
hygiene factors 154–6

Iacocca, Lee 7
image consultants 7
immigration 145, 150–1
imperfections, successful
    leaders 29–30, 40, 157–60,
    204–5, 213–14, 236–9
incentive schemes,
    concepts 180–1, 192–3

income contrasts, capital
      growth 53, 231–2
income-distribution
      statistics 2–4
The Independent 232–3
Independent Data Services 56
India
   middle class consumption 100
   trust surveys 11
individual personal effectiveness
      programmes, solutions 226
individualistic cultures 45–6,
      91–7, 100–1, 159–60,
      206–28
Indonesia, trust surveys 11
industrial leadership discourses,
      concepts 23–6
the Industrial Revolution 21
inflation levels 190
The Inner Game 225
'inner space' 32
innovation drivers 50–1, 132,
      175, 225
inspiration aims, leaders 38
instant gratification, 'lifestyle'
      emergence 4–5, 44–66, 80
institutional investors 52–4,
      64–5, 67–8, 69–74, 91–2,
      106–7, 129–35
   statistics 91
institutionalized dissent 209, 223
insurance companies 52–3, 58–9,
      81–8, 91–2

intangible success
      measures 113–14
integrity 117–18, 121–3, 220,
      230–9
Intel 208
intellectual abilities 28–30
interest rates 71–4, 86–8
introduction 1–12
investment banks 72, 81–8,
      100–1
investment houses, critique 54–5
investment vehicles 52–3
investors
   decision-making 112–14,
      128–35, 198–9
   speculators 50–4, 73–4, 96–7
   types 52, 67–8, 71–2, 91–2
IPPR 46
IQ, performance issues 138
Iraq 62, 236–7
Islam 67
Italy
   enlightened autocrats 25
   executive rewards 57

Japan, executive rewards 57, 58
jargon 32–5, 161–3, 204–6
Jews 67
Job 67
job satisfiers/dissatisfiers 154–6
John Lewis 196
John Madejski Centre for
      Reputation 102, 104–5

Johnson, Ben 4
Jones, Gareth 209–10
Joseph II of Austria (AD 1741–
  1790) 20
Jung, Carl 24, 30
... *Justified Sinner* (Hogg) 35

Kanter, Rosabeth Moss 220
Keillor, Garrison 200–1
Kennedy dynasty 24
Kennedy, John F. 24, 41, 43
Klein, Naomi 230
'knowledge workers' 172–3
KPIs 161, 192–3
Kraft 65–6, 230

Labour government 76
'Lake Wobegon Effect' 200–1,
  236–7
Law, John 51
lawyers 72, 94–5
Lay, Kenneth 4, 220
leaders
  appointments 16–17, 79,
    130–1, 137–8, 170–2
  art history 16–23
  bad leaders 7–8, 10–12,
    39–40, 58–60, 61–2
  brands 212–15, 220, 222, 225
  business books 5–6, 25–6,
    31–5, 208–28
  characteristics 7–9, 10,
    18–19, 21–2, 24–5, 27–30,

  34–5, 108–10, 203–28,
    233–9
co-leaders 208–9
communication skills 28–30,
    36–8, 145–6, 149–50,
    218–19, 221–2, 223, 238–9
company rankings 7–8, 78, 172
competencies 27–30, 33–4,
    109–10, 122–3, 148,
    157–60, 204–8, 237–9
conclusion 229–39
confidence in leaders 1–2,
    4–5, 9–10, 12, 39–40,
    101, 104–5, 107–10,
    116–17, 121–3, 209–28,
    229–39
conflicts of interest 64–5,
    69–74, 89–97
conformity dangers 30, 31–5,
    236–9
critique 1–12, 24–6,
    29–34, 54–7, 65–6,
    118–23, 127–8, 202–28,
    229–39
decision-making 49, 60,
    140–1, 198–9, 221–2,
    224–5, 227–8
definition 36–8, 120–3, 135
deities 16, 17–19, 23–4,
    203–4, 206–7
development issues 15–26,
    135, 142–3, 147–8, 154–6,
    164–5, 209–28, 235–9

dynasties 18, 24–5

egoistic aspects 7–8, 11–12,
    138–40, 202–3

the elect 34–5

The Enlightenment 20–1

environmental issues 15,
    44–66, 67–97, 169–70

ethical values 10, 39–40, 60–1,
    63, 70–4, 121–3, 144–5,
    198–9, 203–28, 230–9

failure reasons 122–3, 146,
    203–4, 206–7, 238–9

followers 122–3, 209–10,
    237–9

future prospects 145–6,
    202–28

globalization drives 9–10,
    37–8, 52–3, 95–6, 119–20,
    131–2, 231–9

heroic leaders 41–2, 208–28

historical background 15–43,
    231–2

human needs/wants 41–3,
    98–9, 122–3, 198–9,
    202–3, 228, 237–9

human weaknesses 6–7, 12,
    29–30, 50–1, 157–60,
    213–15, 237–9

humanity-improvement
    aims 38, 60–1, 189

imperfections 29–30, 40,
    157–60, 204–5, 213–14,
    236–9

jargon 32–5, 161–3, 204–6

lessons learned 5–6, 10–11,
    26, 30, 64–5, 67–8, 87–8,
    127–8

'lifestyle' emergence 2–5, 7–8,
    44–66, 80, 99–100

management contrasts 36–8,
    90–1

modern concepts 23–6

moral philosophers 8–9, 61–3,
    77–8, 120–3

motivations 27–30, 38, 154–6,
    198–9, 207–28

narcissists 7–8, 11–12, 55–6,
    58–60, 66, 95–7, 138–9

objectives 38, 60–3, 82–3,
    98–123, 134–5, 140–1,
    145–6, 162–3, 202–28

parent roles 19, 23

'perfect' leaders 6–7, 29–30,
    31–5, 157, 213–14, 236–9

power 10–12, 19–20, 37–8,
    39–40, 98–101, 122–3,
    131–2

public contempt 4–5, 9–10,
    11–12, 174–5, 228, 229–39

public wants 41–3, 98–123,
    228, 237–9

remuneration reports 64–5,
    96, 167–70

Renaissance art 16–19

scientific management 25–6,
    27

self-image enhancements 7–8, 11–12, 16–17, 21–3, 39–40, 44–66

sin perspectives 6–7

solutions 6–7, 12, 38, 118–23, 127–35, 136–65, 189–201, 202–28, 233–9

stewardship issues 67, 89–97, 112–14, 134–5, 168–70, 215, 217–19, 232–9

successful leaders 1, 26, 27–30, 37–8, 119–23, 134–5, 207–28, 233–9

trust in leaders 1–2, 9–12, 38, 61–2, 69–70, 101, 103–4, 107–10, 116–17, 121–3, 228

weak leaders 1–12, 39–40, 58–60, 61–2

wealth-creation aims 38, 60–1, 82–3, 98–123, 128–9, 189, 216–28, 233–9

'leadership apart' leaders 203–4

Leadership Brand (Ulrich and Smallwood) 212–13

leadership gurus 6, 31–5, 48–9

Leading the Revolution (Hamel) 50

Lee, Stephen 108–9

legalistic responses to business pressures 231–2

Lehman Brothers 40, 188

Lessons from the Teaching of Merlin (Chopra) 32

lessons learned

    bank misperceptions 63–4, 67–8, 87–8, 127–8, 174–5

    leaders 5–6, 10–11, 26, 30, 64–5, 87–8, 127–8

    politics 5–6

leveraged buyouts (LBOs) 71–4

Lewis, Kenneth D. 4

liability losses 67, 81–97

'lifestyle' emergence

    concepts 2–12, 44–66, 80, 99–100

    definition 47–8, 99

limited liability partnerships (LLPs)

    concepts 80–2, 94–7, 131

    definition 94

line managers

    development issues 164–5, 212–13

    engagement 142–5, 161–3

    importance 142–5, 161–3, 212–13

    performance management 161–3, 179

Linksy, Marty 237

liquidity 52–3, 71–4

listening skills 145–6

LLPs *see* limited liability partnerships

local communities 102–7, 203, 239

London School of Economics 69

long-term investment funds 93,
    221–2
L'Oreal generation 4, 44–66, 78,
    83–4, 98, 202, 214,
    233–4, 236
    critique 4, 44–66, 78, 83–4,
        98, 202, 214, 233–4, 236
    definition 4, 44–5, 65–6
    politics 45–7
    revenge aspects 5
    risk-free attitudes 65–6
    success measures 47–9
loss-averse behaviours 199
Louis XIV, King of France 19,
    22, 208

Ma, Jack 7
McClelland, David 27–8
MacDonalds 230
Machiavelli 18–19, 23–4, 30, 237
McKinsey & Co. 48–9, 136–8,
    141–3, 144, 147, 204
Madoff, Bernie 4
makeovers 47–8
management consultants 34–5,
    48–9, 111
management contrasts,
    leaders 36–8, 90–1
Mandela, Nelson 207
Mann, Thomas 90
Marakon model 112, 113–14
Marconi 96

market fundamentalism,
    critique 229–39
'market-based' approaches,
    executive rewards 176–9,
    229–39
Marks and Spencer 65
Marshall, George C. 208
Martin, Roger 41–2
Marx, Karl 24, 117, 230
'Mary Poppins' managers 29,
    157, 236–7
Maxwell, Robert 25
MBA programmes 78, 147,
    171–2
media 7, 21–3, 46–7, 71–2, 76,
    102, 104
    Labour government 76
    'puff pieces' 7
    reputations 102, 104
    self-image enhancements
        21–3, 46–7
    Tribune deal 71–2
Medici family 18
mentoring 156, 226
mergers and acquisitions (M&As)
    8, 39–40, 65–6, 130, 133,
    141–2, 220–2, 233–4
merit reviews 178–9, 204
Merrill Lynch 4
Microsoft 208
Middle East peace process 1
Mill, J.S. 61–2

Mills, D. Quinn 69–71, 75–7, 92

Mintzberg, Henry 203–4

mission 149

Missouri Madness, France 51, 73

Mitterand dynasty 24

mobile workers 145–6

modern leadership discourses,
    concepts 23–6

monarchs, art history 16–23

monopolies 172–3

moral authority, concepts 121–3

moral philosophers, leadership
    explorations 8–9, 61–3,
    77–8, 120–3

mortgage markets, credit
    crunch 81–8

Moses 31

motivations, leaders 27–30, 38,
    154–6, 198–9, 207–28

MP expenses scandal, UK 35,
    214–15

multinational corporations,
    activists/campaigners against
    globalization 119–20,
    230–1

Murdoch, Rupert 4, 76–7

museums, critique 70

mutual funds 92

mutual sector
    deregulated financial services
        81–8
    historical background 82–3

narcissists 7–8, 11–12, 48–50,
    55–6, 58–61, 66, 95–7,
    138–9
    decision-making 49, 60
    Enron 49–50, 58–9
    executive rewards 55–6, 58,
        60–1
    leaders 7–8, 11–12, 55–6,
        58–60, 66, 95–7, 138–9
    talent wars 48–50, 55–6,
        138–9

National Health Service 45, 110

nationalism drivers 37–8

negative employees, effects
    150–1

Nestlé 230

Netherlands, tulipomania 50–1,
    73

networks 28, 46–66, 145–6, 236

The New Capitalists (Davis,
    Lukomnik, Pitt-
    Watson) 39–40, 105–6

New York Attorney General 88

new-age management
    hokum 31–5, 204–6

NGOs 102, 239

Nightingale, Florence 207

non-executive directors
    appointment reforms 130–1,
        167–8, 228
    critique 87–8, 130–1, 195,
        215, 217–19, 228

solutions 130–1, 167–8, 195,
    215, 217–19, 228, 235–6
non-profit organizations,
    critique 70, 77–9
Norse legends, art history 18
North America 2–5, 71,
    96, 150–1, 169–70,
    176, 181, 217–18, 220–2,
    226
  'lifestyle' emergence 2–5
  private equity houses 71, 96
Northern Rock 82–3, 85–6, 230
'Now People' 46–7

Obama, President 5, 75
objectives, leaders 38, 60–3,
    82–3, 98–123, 134–5,
    140–1, 145–6, 162–3,
    202–28
obsessions with details/
    perfectionism 39–40
OECD 57
oligopolies 171
on-line marketplace 116–17
one-minute managers 31
O'Neil, Stan 4
options pricing 182–3
organizational leadership,
    development issues 224–5,
    233–9
organizations 7, 23, 26, 32,
    59–60, 61, 66, 76–7, 89–90,
    93, 101–7, 113–14, 118–23,
    131–2, 139–40, 145–6,
    202–28, 229–39
activists/campaigners against
    globalization 119–20,
    230–1
alignment benefits 139–40,
    203–4, 227–8
authentic business 121–3,
    127–35, 210–28, 233–9
commitment 139–40, 142–5,
    150–1, 221–8
core purpose of the
    organization 149, 162,
    202–3, 224–5, 227–8
engagement 139–48, 150–1,
    155–6, 209–28
feudal-court analogy 7, 23
future prospects 145–6,
    202–28
narcissistic leaders 7–8,
    11–12, 55–6, 58–60, 66,
    95–7, 138–9
rankings 7, 78, 172
reform needs 12, 64–5, 68–74,
    96–7, 100–1, 127–35,
    136–45, 189–201, 211–28,
    229–30, 233–9
reputations 61, 76–7, 89–90,
    93, 101–7, 113–14, 119–23,
    130, 214–28, 239
sizes of organizations 131–5
talent wars 48–51, 54–6,
    63–4, 68, 77–80, 135,

136–65, 168–70, 171–5,
200–1, 204–28, 232–9
values 118–23, 141–5, 211–28
O'Rourke, P.J. 114–15, 183
overview of the book 6–7,
11–12
owner controls 52–4, 64–5, 67,
81–97, 102–7, 128–35,
170–201, 215–28, 232–9
Ozymandias 132–3

Pakenhams dynasty 24
parent roles, leaders 19, 23
Parmalat 25, 230
Patel, Raj 229
peer reviews 221–2
penalties, 'gods' that failed 5
pension funds 52–4, 67–8, 91–2,
96, 129, 186–7
perfect competition 117, 171
'perfect' leaders 6–7, 29–30,
31–5, 157, 213–14, 236–9
performance issues 56–7, 82–3,
108–10, 111–14, 135,
138–65, 168–70, 178–81,
190–3
above average performance
112–14
alignment benefits 139–40,
203–4, 227–8
benchmarking 32, 111–14,
190–1, 200–1, 204–6
coaching 156, 225

commitment 139–40, 142–5,
150–1
engagement 139–48, 150–1
enhancement methods 139–44
executive rewards 56–7, 82–3,
135, 168–70, 178–81, 190–1,
192–3, 199, 200–1, 222, 234
HR systems 161–3, 204, 212
IQ 138
line managers 161–3, 179
negative employees 150–1
poor performers 144, 178–9,
181, 193, 222
standards 108–10, 116–17,
129–35, 203–6, 225
statistics 56–7
talent wars 136–65
triple bottom line 192–3
performance reviews 28–9, 148,
157–63, 178–9, 190–1,
204
Pericles 24
personal debt, statistics 84–5
Peters, Tom 32
Petrarch 24
Plato 23–4
political fundamentalism 1
political gods, 'gods' that failed 4–5,
25–6, 67–8, 117–18
politics
celebrity cultures 2–5, 7–8,
59–60
conflicts of interest 70–4

critique 2–9, 25–6, 61–3,
    98–9, 117–20, 127–35,
    229–39
donors 70–1, 75–80, 134
enlightened autocrats 25
lessons learned 5–6
L'Oreal generation 45–7
public contempt 4–5, 9–10,
    11–12, 174–5, 228, 229–30
public policy agendas 109–10,
    118–20, 122–3, 127–35,
    159–60, 228
society 61–2, 70–1, 75–80,
    118–21, 127–35, 230–9
poor performers 144, 178–9,
    181, 193, 222
the Pope 23–4
Porras, Jerry 149
Porsche 53–4
Porter, Michael 112
portraiture, historical
    background 16–17
potential of employees 146–7
poverty 119–20
power 10–12, 19–20, 37–8,
    39–40, 98–101, 122–3,
    128–35
    abuses 10–12, 39–40, 122–3,
        131–2
    corruption 62–3, 75–80,
        229–30
    leadership needs 37–8
    Monarchs 19–20

shareholders 129–35
surveys 10–12
pressure groups 104
prices
    economic theory 170–5
    value of leadership 229–39
private equity houses
    concepts 71–4, 96
    critique 71–2, 96
    statistics 71
pro-activity jargon 32
professionalism needs 69–71
property-owning
    democracies 2–4
Prosser, David 232–3
prudence 21–2
Prudential 233
psychological effects of
    success 58–9
public contempt, leaders 4–5,
    9–10, 11–12, 174–5, 228,
    229–39
public expenditure cuts 127
public policy agendas
    concepts 109–10, 118–20,
        122–3, 127–35, 159–60, 228
    contents 128–32
    solutions 128–35, 228
public relations (PR) 21–3, 222
public sector, salaries 173–4,
    177–8, 190–1
public sector net debt (PSND) 85
public services, critique 1–2

public wants, leaders 41–3,
98–123, 228, 237–9
'puff pieces', mass media 7
Putin, Vladimir 25

R&D investments, private equity
houses 71
radical change, reform needs 12,
64–5, 68–74, 96–7, 100–1,
128–35, 189–201, 229–30,
233–9
Rand, Ayn 4
rankings, organizations 7, 78, 172
rational thinking 15–16, 24,
25–6, 41–3, 112–14,
116–17, 198–9, 214–15
re-engineering jargon 32, 161–3,
204–6
Reagan, Ronald 2
recognition, Herzberg
model 155–6
recruitment consultants 177–9
recruitment methods
attitude factors 150–1
internal/external
candidates 152–3
talent wars 137–8, 171–5, 234–5
reform needs 12, 64–5, 68–74,
96–7, 100–1, 127–35,
136–45, 189–201, 211–28,
229–30, 233–9
banks 64–5, 72–4, 96–7,
100–1, 229–30

corporate governance 64–5,
96–7, 128–9, 166–70,
215–28
executive rewards 189–201
public policy agendas 127–35
radical change 12, 64–5,
68–74, 96–7, 100–1,
128–35, 189–201, 229–30,
233–9
structures 127–35, 210–28
success measures 100–1
regulators 2–3, 9, 11–12,
52, 54–5, 66, 67–8,
81–8, 92–4, 116–18, 177,
230–9
critique 2–3, 9, 52, 54–5, 66,
67–8, 116–18, 230–9
deregulated financial
services 2–3, 52, 54–5, 66,
81–8, 92–4, 117–18, 177
executive rewards 166–70,
238–9
historical background 116
needs 116–18, 238–9
surveys 11–12
relativity principle, executive
rewards 196, 235
reliability 21–2, 117–18
religions 1, 6–7, 16, 17–18, 34,
63, 67–8
critique 70
education systems 7
fundamentalism 1

new-age management
    hokum 31–5
power of the Christian
    church 17–18
sin perspectives 6–7
remuneration consultants 176–7
remuneration reports
    concepts 64–5, 96, 129–30,
    167–8, 191, 194
Renaissance art 16–19
Renaissance leadership discourses,
    concepts 23–6
reputations 61, 76–7, 89–90, 93,
    101–7, 113–14, 119–23,
    127–8, 130, 204–28, 239
    definition 102–3
    drivers 102–7, 119, 216–28,
    239
    EP/EVA
        considerations 113–14
    reporting reforms 130
    'The SPIRIT' reputation
        model 102–4
    stakeholders 102–7, 113–14
rescue packages, banks 73, 87–8,
    106–7, 127–8
research and publish drives,
    business schools 26
resignations 155–6
resource allocations,
    concepts 112–14, 170–1
responsibilities 41–3, 60–1, 67,
    70–4, 90–7, 127–8,

134–5, 155–6, 215, 216–28,
    232–9
Herzberg model 155–6
stewardship issues 67, 90–7,
    134–5, 215, 217–19, 232–9
retail banks 80–8, 113–14
retained amounts, bonuses 193
retirement schemes
    concepts 186–7
returns 52–3, 65–6, 73–4,
    81–8, 89–90, 94–5,
    96–7, 111–14, 137–8,
    224–5
    definition 111
    fund managers 93
    risk attitudes 65–6, 73–4,
    81–8, 89–90, 94–5
    speculators 52–3, 96–7
revolutions 18, 19
Richelieu, Cardinal 208
right and wrong, concepts 61–3,
    123, 214–15, 238–9
risk attitudes 65–6, 73–4, 81–8,
    89–90, 94–5
    entrepreneurs 89–90
    LLPs 94–5
risk management 80–97,
    218–19, 230–9
risk registers 161
risk-free attitudes
    credit crunch 73–4
    deregulated financial
        services 81–8

executive rewards 65–6, 82–3,
    86–8, 185
Robbins, Anthony 32
Robinson, Sir Gerry 7
rock icons, celebrity cultures 5
role models, self-reinforcing
    celebrity role models 5, 7–8,
    59–60, 206–7, 208–28,
    232–3, 236–9
Romanovs 19
Roosevelt, Eleanor 33
Royal Air Force 137–8
Royal Bank of Scotland (RBS),
    critique 8, 63, 230
rule-breaking bad leaders 39–40
Russia 25, 100, 146

J Sainsbury 65
salaries 56, 173–4, 176–9,
    190–1
    graduates 178
    options proportion in executive
        rewards 56
    public sector 173–4, 177–8,
        190–1
    reviews 178–9, 190–1
    solutions 190–1
    statistics 176–9, 190–1
    talent wars 56, 173–4, 176–9
'salary clubs' 176–7
Sarbanes-Oxley Act 2002 96
'Say on Pay' legislation 167–8
scarce resources

concepts 2, 99–100, 133–4,
    173–5, 227
    executive rewards 173–5
Schaefer, Scott 200–1
Schein, Edgar 211
Scholes, Myron S. 182–3
scientific management 25–6, 27
Scout Movement 80
Second World War 137
self-awareness aspects of moral
    authority 121–3, 221–2
self-belief aspects of moral
    authority 121–3
self-centeredness 45–66, 95–7,
    100–1, 138–40, 202–3, 210–28
self-confidence 28–30, 33–4,
    49–50, 121–3, 209–28
self-controls 221–2
self-doubts 122–3
self-expectations 198–9
self-help industry 31–2
self-image enhancements,
    leaders 7–8, 11–12, 16–17,
    21–3, 39–40, 44–66
self-promotion aspects
    Enron 49–50
    L'Oreal generation 46–66
self-reinforcing celebrity role
    models 5, 7–8, 59–60,
    206–7, 208–28, 232–3,
    236–9
self-styled leadership gurus 6,
    31–5

self-worth 44–66, 95–7
selfishness, narcissistic
        leaders 59–60, 95–7,
        138–9
sensitivity aims, leaders 38
service centres 212–13
Shakespeare, William 24, 30, 74,
        90
share brokers, deregulated
        financial services 81–2
share options 40, 55–7, 182–5,
        194, 201
    critique 40, 55–7, 182–5,
        194
    solutions 194, 201
    statistics 56–7
shareholder value
    concepts 53, 65–6, 100–1,
        111–23, 137–8, 224–5,
        229–39
    definition 111–12
shareholders 52–4, 64–5, 81–97,
        102–7, 111–23, 128–35,
        203–28, 239
    activism 64–5, 106–7, 128–9,
        167–8, 184–5
    conflicts of interest 64–5,
        69–74, 95–7
    institutional investors 52–4,
        64–5, 67–8, 69–74, 91–2,
        106–7, 129–35
    powers 129–35
Sherlock Holmes 208

shopping
    'lifestyle' emergence 2–5,
        44–66, 99–100
short selling (shorting), critique
        53–4
short-termism 70–4, 102–4,
        106–7, 181, 192–3, 221–2,
        238–9
Simon, Paul 136
sin perspectives 6–7
Sirota, David 140, 143
'situational leadership' 209
sizes of organizations, reform
        needs 131–5
Skinner, B.F. 24
Smallwood, Norm 212–13
Smith, Adam 112, 114–15
'social capital' skills 145–6
social powers
    historical background
        20–1
    markets 122–3
social science research 27–30,
        206–7
socialism 117, 229–30, 234–5
society
    art as a mirror 22–3
    business conflicts 70–4,
        75–80, 132, 174–5, 189,
        220–2, 228, 229–39
    demographic changes 145–6
    politics 61–2, 70–1, 75–80,
        118–21, 127–35, 230–9

values 10–12, 23–4, 43, 44–5,
    60–1, 70–4, 75–80,
    118–21, 170, 198–9, 220–8
solutions 6–7, 12, 38, 118–23,
    127–35, 136–65, 189–201,
    202–28, 233–9
    authentic business 121–3,
        127–35, 210–28, 233–9
    boards of directors 215, 217–19,
        224–5, 227–8, 235–6
    chairmen 218–19
    collaborative approaches
        128–35, 145–6, 150–1,
        192–3, 202–3, 207–28
    commitment 139–40, 142–5,
        150–1, 221–8
    competency assessment
        problems 157–60, 204–5,
        237–9
    core purpose of the
        organization 149, 162,
        202–3, 224–5, 227–8
    development contracts 154–6
    engagement 139–48, 150–1,
        155–6, 209–28
    executive rewards 135, 189–
        201, 227, 235–9
    fund managers 129, 134–5,
        197, 239
    HR systems 161–3, 204, 212
    imperfect leaders 29–30, 40,
        157–60, 204–5, 213–14,
        236–9
    individual personal
        effectiveness programmes
        226
    internal/external recruitment
        candidates 152–3
    leaders 6–7, 12, 38, 118–23,
        127–35, 136–65, 189–201,
        202–28, 233–9
    line managers 142–5, 161–3,
        212–13
    organizational
        leadership 224–5, 233–9
    public policy agendas 128–35,
        159–60, 228
    recruitment for attitude 150–1
    talent wars 135, 136–65, 234–9
    values 220–8
Sophocles 24
sourcing decisions 234
South Sea Bubble, UK 51–2, 73
speculators
    critique 50–4, 73–4, 96–7
spin doctors 7
'The SPIRIT' reputation
    model 102–4
spiritual/material aspects, well-
    being 7, 32–3, 39–40,
    58–9, 230–1
sponsorship 76, 134
sport gods, 'gods' that failed 4
sports stars, celebrity cultures 5,
    208
Sprint 39–40

stakeholders
  behaviours towards
    businesses 102–5
  concepts 102–10,
    111–12, 128–35, 203–28,
    232–9
  emotions towards
    businesses 102–3
  experiences of
    businesses 102–3,
    108–10
  performance
    enhancements 140
  reforms 128–35
  reputations 102–7, 113–14,
    130
  types 102–3, 105, 111–12,
    203, 232, 239
  voting reforms 129–35
standards 108–10, 116–17,
    129–35, 203–6, 225
Star Trek the Next Generation (tv
    series) 31
stewardship issues
  concepts 67, 89–97, 112–14,
    134–5, 168–70, 215,
    217–19, 232–9
  definition 90–1, 96
  entrepreneurship
    distinctions 90, 96, 217–19,
    232, 239
Stewart, Martha 4
stock lending, critique 53–4

strategic capabilities,
    concepts 112–14, 122–3,
    158–9
strategic goals 224–5
strengths and weaknesses,
    competencies 28–30, 33–4,
    157–60, 204–5
structures
  critique 1–2, 9, 25, 66, 68,
    81–90, 92–4, 122–3,
    127–35, 169–70, 210–28
  deregulated financial
    services 2–3, 52, 54–5, 66,
    81–8, 92–4, 117–18, 177
  future prospects 145–6,
    202–28
  reform needs 127–35, 210–28
style gods, 'gods' that failed 4
success measures
  L'Oreal generation 47–9
  negative aspects 58–9
  reform needs 100–1, 233–9
  reputations 61, 76–7, 89–90,
    93, 101–7, 113–14,
    119–23, 127–8, 130,
    204–28, 239
successful leaders 1, 26, 27–30,
    37–8, 119–23, 134–5,
    207–28, 233–9
Sugar, Lord of Clapton 7
suppliers 102–7, 234, 239
  see also stakeholders
Sweden, executive rewards 57

Switzerland
    executive rewards 57–8
    'Voice of the People' survey
        (2008) 10
symbolism, art history 16–23
synergies 220–2
systems, critique 1–2, 9, 25, 66,
    67–8, 211–28, 239

takeovers 8, 39–40, 65–6, 130,
    133, 233–4
talent wars 48–51, 54–6, 63–4,
    68, 77–80, 135, 136–65,
    168–70, 171–5, 200–1,
    204–28, 232–9
    critique 48–50, 54–6, 63–4,
        77–80, 135, 136–40, 146–8,
        171–5, 200–1, 204–28,
        232–9
    definition 48, 142, 206–7
    engagement 139–48, 150–1
    executive rewards 48–50,
        54–6, 63–4, 135,
        168–70, 171–9, 200–1,
        232–9
    'Lake Wobegon Effect' 200–1,
        236–7
    narcissists 48–50, 55–6, 138–9
    public sector salaries 173–4
    recruitment methods 137–8,
        171–5, 234–5
    salaries 56, 173–4, 176–9
    solutions 135, 136–65, 234–9

statistics 137, 138–9, 147–8,
    168–70
taxes 40, 95, 127, 130–1, 189,
    201, 234
Taylor, F.W. 25–6
teams
    bonuses 192–3, 223
    development issues 224–5
    institutionalized dissent 209,
        223
    successful teams 27–30, 40,
        42–3, 202–28
technological advances,
    globalization drives 37–8
television/radio, self-image
    enhancements 21–2
terminology contrasts,
    jargon 34–5
terrorism 10
Tesco 65
Testelin, Henri (AD
    1616–1695) 19
Thatcher, Margaret 2, 84
Thiam, Tidjane 233
The Times 155
tobacco sponsorship 76
'Together' loan, Northern
    Rock 85–6
'toxic debt' 77–80
tracker funds 93
trade unions 176
trading instincts of
    humans 114–16

training courses 36–8, 135,
  164–5, 224–5, 226, 236
transparency needs 69–71,
  122–3, 129–35, 176–9, 191,
  192–3, 215–28, 231, 232–9
trend-following 'lifestyle'
  emergence 4–5
Tribune deal 71–2
triple bottom line 192–3
Trump, Donald 7
trust 1–2, 9–12, 21–3, 38, 61–2,
  69–70, 101, 102–4, 107–10,
  116–17, 121–3, 223, 228
  concepts 1–2, 9–12, 69–70,
    101, 102–4, 107–10,
    116–17, 121–3, 228
  definition 108–9
  problems 1–2, 9–12, 69–70,
    108–9, 228
  surveys 9–10, 11, 108–9
tulipomania, Netherlands 50–1,
  73
Turner, Ted 4
Tyco 96, 230

UK 2, 4–5, 7–8, 11, 19, 22, 25,
  27, 33, 44–6, 55–8, 64–5,
  69–72, 81–97, 117–18,
  128–35, 145, 166–70,
  178–9, 206–7, 230–1
  BP 132–3, 230, 232
  British Values Survey 45–6
  coalition government 77

corporate governance 64–5,
  96, 128–35, 166–70, 230–1
deregulated financial
  services 2–3, 52, 54–5, 66,
  81–8, 92–4, 117–18
enlightened autocrats 25
executive rewards 55–8,
  69–70, 86–8, 96–7, 178–9,
  186–7
institutional investors 91
LLPs 94–5, 131
'Most Admired Companies'
  awards 7–8
MP expenses scandal 35,
  214–15
personal debt statistics 84–5
private equity houses 71, 96
remuneration reports 64–5,
  96–7, 129–30, 167–70
retirement schemes 186–7
Royal Air Force 137
South Sea Bubble 51–2, 73
surveys 11, 45–6, 155–8
trade union influences 176
trust surveys 11
Ulrich, Dave 212–13
United States 2–5, 6, 10–11,
  27–8, 32–3, 43, 51, 55–8,
  64–5, 69–71, 73, 86–8,
  94–7, 98–101, 110, 117–18,
  150–1, 168–70, 200–1, 206,
  236–7
  bank rescues 73, 87–8

BP 132–3, 230, 232
business books 6, 31–5
corporate governance 96
executive rewards 55–8,
    69–70, 96–7, 186–7
health care 195
institutional investors 91
'Lake Wobegon Effect' 200–1,
    236–7
'lifestyle' emergence 2–5
LLPs 94–5
mortgage market 86–8
private equity houses 71–2
retirement schemes 186–7
Sarbanes-Oxley Act 2002 96
self-help industry 31–2
Senate Banking
    Committee 87–8
trade union influences 176
trust surveys 10, 11
universities, critique 70, 77–9
unlimited liability
    partnerships 81–2

value chains 100–1
value-creation 2, 110, 111–23,
    175, 224–5, 229–39
    activists/campaigners against
        globalization 119–20
    concepts 111–23, 175, 224–5
    goods and services 2
values 10–12, 23–4, 39–40,
    43, 44–66, 70–4,

98–123, 141–3, 198–9,
    203–28
    breaches 220–2
    British Values Survey 45–6
    codes of conduct 222
    definitions 114–15, 118, 220,
        227
    L'Oreal generation 4, 44–66,
        98, 214, 233–4, 236
    organizations 118–23, 141–5,
        211–28
    society 10–12, 23–4, 43,
        44–5, 60–1, 70–4, 75–80,
        118–21, 170, 198–9, 220–8
    solutions 220–8
    value contrasts 114–15
variable reward structures
    concepts 180–1, 192–3
    solutions 192–3
venture capitalists, critique 70–1
'virtuous' leaders 8–9
vision 32–3, 43, 120, 121–3,
    149, 158–9, 174–5, 203–4,
    207–28
'Voice of the People' survey
    (2008) 9–10
Volkswagen (VW) 53–4
'voodoo' 31–5
voting reforms 129–35

'Wackygate' 32–3
Walker Review on corporate
    governance 64–5

Wall Street Journal 171–2
Wall-Mart 169
Warhol, Andy 236
warm gestures, cold showers 189,
    201
weak leaders 1–12, 39–40,
    58–60, 61–2
The Wealth of Nations
    (Smith) 114–15
wealth-creation 38, 60–1, 82–3,
    98–123, 128–9, 175,
    216–28, 233–9
    activists/campaigners against
        globalization 119–20
    methods 115
the wealthy, critique 2–4
Weber, Max 24
Welch, Jack 7, 31
well-being, spiritual/material
    aspects 7, 32–3, 39–40,
    58–9, 230–1
Wheen, Francis 31–2
whistleblowers 222
Whyte, Jamie 34
Wilde, Oscar 229
Williamson, Marianne 32
Woods, Tiger 4
Woolard, Edward S., Jr 200–1
workforce
    core purpose of the
        organization 149, 162,
        202–3, 224–5, 227–8

demographic changes 145–6
development issues 146–7,
    154–6, 164–5, 235–9
diversity benefits 30, 159–60,
    202–3, 207–28, 237–9
hygiene factors 154–6
immigration 145, 150–1
job satisfiers/
    dissatisfiers 154–6
loyalties 146, 147, 154–6, 203,
    221–2, 239
motivations 154–6, 198–9,
    207–28
potential of employees 146–7
resignations 155–6
retention drivers 146, 147,
    176–7, 203, 213, 235
World Economic Forum 9–10,
    11
WorldCom 4, 25, 39–40, 96,
    147, 188, 230
worthy goals/actions,
    concepts 61–3, 123

yuppie symbols of the
    1980s 50–1

Zapatistas 230
Ziglar, Zig 32